The Struggling Writer

Strategies to Help Kids Focus, Build Stamina, and Develop Writing Confidence

Janet Angelillo

◀▌SCHOLASTIC

New York · Toronto · London · Auckland · Sydney
Mexico City · New Delhi · Hong Kong · Buenos Aires

Credits

Page 57: From PRAIRIE TRAIN by Marsha Wilson Chall. Text copyright © 2003 by Marsha Wilson Chall. Used with permission of the Author and BookStop Literary Agency, LLC. All rights reserved.

Page 57: From ROSA by Nikki Giovanni. Copyright © 2005 by Nikki Giovanni. Reprinted by permission of Henry Holt and Company, LLC.

Page 58: Reprinted with the permission of Simon & Schuster Books for Young Readers, an imprint of Simon & Schuster Children's Publishing Division from SALT IN HIS SHOES: Michael Jordan in Pursuit of a Dream by Deloris Jordan with Roslyn M. Jordan. Text copyright © 2000 by Deloris Jordan and Roslyn M. Jordan.

Editor: Lois Bridges

Production editor: Gloria Pipkin

Copy editor: David Klein

Cover design: Jorge J. Namerow

Interior design: Sydney Wright

ISBN-13: 978-0-545-05896-4

ISBN-10: 0-545-05896-1

Contents

Acknowledgments

It's a common, romantic myth that writers create their books wearing their pajamas and slippers, in neat, cozy, well-lighted rooms, away from long commutes and demanding co-workers. They spend their time sipping coffee, dreaming up stories, and keeping only a dog for company. The truth of it is quite different. Professional books are not written without visiting schools, libraries, and classrooms, or without crisscrossing the country to talk to many people, to attend conferences, and to iron out details. To borrow an old saying, it takes a network. And so, with respect to my ever-faithful dog, here are the names of people all over the country I wish to thank.

First, I must thank my stellar friend and patient editor, Lois Bridges. She waited longer for this book than I have excuses to give! Her wise comments and gentle phone calls are always welcome. Frankly, she makes me a better writer, and that's what the best editors do. I also thank the entire production staff at Scholastic. Their work is professional, thorough, and whole-heartedly dedicated to producing the best work for teachers.

Thanks always to Lucy Calkins. The Teachers College Reading and Writing Project has changed more teaching lives and children's learning than any other institution I know. Without it, I don't know who I would be as a teacher.

Thanks to my colleagues and friends, and to the brilliant people in literacy education who have made me think differently: Carl Anderson, Ralph Fletcher, Ruth Culham, Laura Robb, Katie Ray, Linda Rief, Lester Laminack, Isoke Nia, Shirley McPhillips, Michael Shaw, Jim Blasingame.

To the administrators and teachers all over the country who work so wisely for the children in their care: Pam Dalton, Christine Pruss, David Krafick, Laura Kaddis, Pamela Ebersole-Buckley, and Priscilla Eller in Danbury, Connecticut; Israel Soto, Lorraine Hasty, Betty Lugo, and Angela Camiolo at PS 57 in East Harlem, New York; Mindy Hoffar and Julia Nixon of All Write in Fort Wayne, Indiana; Frances Castillo, Hazel Cruz, Olga

The Struggling Writer

Tsoupros, and Susan Ottomanelli of PS 83 in East Harlem, New York; Andrea Hernandez, at The Bilingual Bicultural Mini School in East Harlem; as well as teachers in Chicago, El Paso, Las Cruces, Providence, Boston, Albany, Brooklyn, and East Orange, and in every state.

To Father Gregory Noel, OFM Cap, and to my dear friends at Seton, with endless gratitude and humility.

And to my family. Charles, Cheryl, Mark, Alex—you are forever there for me with love and gentle support, always nudging me. God bless you.

Introduction

I was a struggling writer

When I grew up in the 1950s and '60s, writing instruction was as unsophisticated as could be. The teacher assigned a topic on Monday, and by Friday, we handed in neat final copies for a grade and corrections in red ink. Good writing consisted of good spelling and handwriting; bad writing was anything else. Since I struggled with spelling and handwriting, I fell in the "bad writer" category. At home, I easily produced stories on yellow paper that I hid in a drawer, but at school, I was mediocre at best. I knew it by the frown my writing produced on teachers' faces—my writing was pretty bad. The truth is that this "teacher judgment," unchecked, could have kept me from college, from teaching, and from the joy of writing all these years. Fortunately, one teacher rescued me with one positive comment, because he had eyes to see. And that made all the difference. Mr. Peck, I thank you.

How far we've come in the teaching of writing, and yet, how much some students still struggle. I know how they feel because I've felt that same confusion, humiliation, anger, and resentment. I remember thinking, "What is it that she wants from me and why can't I do it?" I see this on the faces of strugglers everywhere, and I want to tell them that I know what it's like. And while I would love to claim that one positive comment would change it all for them, the truth is that, for many, it won't. I wanted to write, so I cared about what my English teacher said. If the physical education teacher had given me a positive comment, it might have meant little; I care not one whit about sports and such. So I also understand the difficulty of performing well in an area that holds no interest for students. I couldn't bear to climb ropes, but it was far more painful when my writing didn't work.

This book is divided into two parts. In the first part, each chapter looks at a type of struggler, from the ones who say they hate writing to those who struggle with written conventions. The truth is that most struggling writers are composites of the students in these chapters, for it is rare that a struggler struggles with only one aspect of writing. I encourage you to read through these chapters with your own struggling students in mind and to picture them as cross-sections of each area.

Part II looks at the teaching of struggling writers and the research behind it. I look at some of the struggles students have and why it is so difficult to teach them, at the role of meaningful assessment of writers, and at ways whole-class teaching can address needs of strugglers. Finally, there is the BMW of teaching: conferring. Conferring is the strongest and most challenging work for us. Without a doubt, conferring and small-group work are two types of teaching that can do the most for struggling writers.

Finally, I have come to believe a few important principles about teaching struggling writers, and all students, for that matter. Of course, we must have the energy and wisdom that best-practice teaching brings to the classroom. We must be prepared, well nourished, and rested. We need materials and uninterrupted time, smaller classes and clean surroundings. All these are the basic human rights and requirements for teaching.

But we must also be in a state of mind that allows us to live in a place of gentleness and mercy. Too many teachers are so stressed by school schedules and testing demands that their kindness and compassion is in danger of being lost. No student, especially a struggler, should spend day after day with someone who is disparaging, negative, sarcastic, nasty, judgmental, or mean. Teaching requires that we bring the best of ourselves to class every day and offer it to our students. Hard as this is, even with the best of students, it is what we are called to do. We must do great things every day and small things with great love.

Students who meet with frustration in writing must see us smile at them every day. They must hear kind words and encouragement, and receive recognition of tiny advancements they make. They need gentle voices with calm exteriors so they will internalize that everything will be all right. I believe that the stress high-stakes testing has caused for teachers and youngsters will not be without societal ramifications. We have the opportunity to grow a generation of writers who love writing through authentic instruction, but we risk losing it all to the anguish of tests. We also risk losing our strugglers if we cannot bring thoughtful and loving instruction to writing. To this end, I urge you to audiotape yourself one day and listen to when and if you answer students with anger, annoyance, or condescension. It is more common than we realize because we are more stressed than ever.

Our work reaches the future, as so many have said. We must find something grand inside ourselves that we can draw upon every day, so that our classrooms are places of dignified instruction for all students. Our strugglers must know that their wrestling to write and to understand will yield success. We know they can write with confidence, and that, over time, they will come to believe they can succeed.

Part I

Common Student Struggles and the Teaching That Overcomes Them

In most classrooms, a teacher's eye soon picks out the strugglers. They are the ones who don't have their supplies, dig in their desks for who knows what, amble to the meeting area, have that "deer in headlights" look on their faces, want water or frequent bathroom visits, and, sadly, often are at odds with the teacher. They are the ones about whom teachers sometimes say to me, "Would you work with Greg? I can't do anything with him," or even worse, "I've had it with Marsha. She's all yours." How sad and, frankly, unprofessional. To paraphrase a famous saying, it is not the good students who need brilliant teaching, but the ones who struggle to learn.

Therefore, let's start out by examining several types of struggling writers. I have observed them again and again in classroom after classroom, and I am sure most of you have had them in your classrooms—year after year. I invite you to imagine the students I describe and compare them with students you've had or who are in your class right now. Try the prescriptions I suggest, but also think creatively about how to help these students by thinking of your own struggles and how you work to overcome them. No one can provide the answers to every problem or describe every possible problem. Sometimes, you'll find your students are composites of strugglers. Students are individuals with unique needs. For all of us, life is a journey of rooting out and overcoming difficulty.

1

"I hate writing"

The Reluctant Writer

Since this book is filled with true confessions, here is another one: I hate to exercise. And while I maintain that *hate* is a four-letter word and should be banned as such, I still hate to exercise. Yuck. It's tiring, and sweaty, and boring, and uncomfortable, and . . . you get the gist. Just getting started makes me tired, grumpy, and annoyed at myself. Everyone else at the gym or the track is, well, so good at it. They look sleek and healthy. I feel inadequate, so I flop on a chair and mope. It would take me years to catch up to them, and it just isn't worth the effort. So I procrastinate, lie to my doctor, and eat ice cream instead. (By the way, my doctor is not fooled.)

Don't reluctant writers feel the same way? It's tiring and boring to them. They dread writing time, and because others seem so good at it, this highlights their feelings of inadequacy. They become angry or lethargic. Why even bother?

In this chapter, I will look at two writers who claim to "hate" writing. It seems obvious that something else is going on under their raw emotion, including recollection of experiences when writing was not enjoyable for them. Teachers cannot undo the past experiences of their struggling writers, but they can help them in the present. This chapter will look at the following:

- Students who "hate writing" in general

- Students who hate writing because all writing is teacher-focused

- Students who lack essential tools for writing

Students Who "Hate Writing" in General

I visit a fifth-grade class where the teacher is energetic, smart, and well prepared with rigorous writing instruction. She has "looped" with her students from fourth to fifth grade, so this is the second year they are together. She and I are studying how to teach essay writing, but she tells me on the side that mostly she is worried about Garrett. As with all students, he has tremendous potential. Nevertheless, he balks at her requests and appears ready to fall asleep or fall off his chair when it's time to write.

"Just watch him," she says. "I'd appreciate any advice you can give me on how to help him."

I pull a chair next to him and smile. "How's it going?" I ask, quoting Carl Anderson's famous opening for conferring with students (2000).

Garrett puts his head down on the desk and mumbles. When I lean closer and tell him I can't hear him, he straightens up and yells, "I hate writing!"

I think a lot about Garrett before I return to the class the following week. I think about how he must feel every day, being forced to perform at something he thinks he despises. It's as if I had to exercise every day on demand with someone watching over me and grading me . . . I get the shivers thinking about it. But as much as exercising is good for me, writing is important for Garrett. I begin to think about ways to get myself to exercise and then transpose those strategies to ways to teach Garrett to get over his "hate" of writing. Here's what I list for myself that I hope might help Garrett:

- Stop thinking about other people and their successes and focus on your own work.

- Look at only one challenge at a time so you don't get overwhelmed.

- Plan your work aloud and then try to get at least one thing done that day.

The next time I visit Garrett's class, I tell him about my own struggles. We look at my list and he laughs. "Why don't you just play basketball after school?" he asks.

I smile. "That's what you would do, isn't it?" I shake my head. "It's hard for me. I do anything I can to avoid it."

"Gee," he answers sympathetically. "That's bad. Just go and do it."

Garrett and I talk about how making ourselves do something we don't like is hard, just as writing is hard for him. He reiterates that he hates writing; I reiterate that I hate exercise. Then something happens that I believe is a key to making this work: We look at each other and laugh. We've formed a bond. Garrett sees me as a struggler.

We look at the first point on the list I've made: Stop thinking about other people. I ask Garrett to explain to me how that could help me with exercising, and he points out on his fingers what he's thinking:

- It doesn't matter what other people think or do.
- You do this for yourself and your own fun.
- It doesn't have to look good or be perfect.
- You are practicing to get better at it.

I write down his ideas as quickly as I can. Then I ask him if we can use his ideas to think about his writing. He frowns, but nods.

Garrett admits that when he looks around the class and sees other students writing, he gets discouraged. He feels he can't keep up with them in amount or in quality, so he gives up. I remind him by reading back the points he made to me about exercising, and he shakes his head.

"It's not the same," he says, whining.

"Well, let's imagine for a minute that it is," I answer. "What could you do to stop thinking about what other people are writing so you can focus more on your own work?"

Garrett agrees that he will stand a folder on his desk to block his view of other students. He agrees that he will not care how much they've written, or whether what they write is "better" than his writing. We show his plan to his teacher, who is happily onboard with us. This is the first self-regulatory strategy that Garrett will try (Collins, 1998).

The Struggling Writer

> *Research note:*
>
> Self-regulation is a strategy often used by teachers of special education. It focuses on teaching youngsters to recognize what gets them off-task or what keeps them from getting started. From there, the students work on a plan of two or three simple steps they will follow to keep their work going.

In the research on struggling writers, one important teaching strategy that emerges is self-regulation. Students who struggle often lack ways to get started and to keep on going. Teachers frequently assume that all students can follow through on instructions, and can get prickly when students don't do their work. The research recommends that teachers take time in individual conferences to help students hammer out a plan for keeping themselves working and for celebrating completion of each step. For Garrett, and other students who resist writing in general, these strategies must include getting to the heart of why the student resists. "I hate writing" says much more than "I don't like to do this." It also says: I feel bad about my work or myself, or I'm too tired, hungry, or distracted to think, or I don't trust my thinking, or this is too hard for me, or I don't know what the teacher really wants, and so on. Strategies for building writing performance must be short and doable. They must be cast as self-help and drawn up together with the student, lest they be seen as one more requirement decreed by the teacher. They must also be revisited from time to time, as it is possible to ignore or misuse them. Ultimately, students must "buy in" to working out their struggles, which is why the teacher's honest discussion of his or her struggles is helpful. As I report to Garrett my progress with exercise, he is encouraged to show his progress with writing.

Self-regulation strategies are appropriate in all categories of struggle, including the following in writing:

- Parts of the writing process

- Ways to get started

- Ways to write more on the page

- Ways to stay with a topic

- Ways to fight distraction or procrastination

- Ways to live with something you think you dislike

Over the course of several weeks, I am able to confer with Garrett once a week. Eventually he tells me he doesn't really hate writing, he just hates feeling bad about it. Together we create a list of ways for him to make writing more agreeable. Garrett notes that I could use the list for exercising and says he's going to hold me to it! Notice that it is our relationship—our tiny writing community of two—that makes this all palatable for him.

Here is Garrett's plan for learning to "un-hate" writing:

1. I will measure my writing against my own expectations for myself.

2. Before I write every day, I will be sure I know what to expect of myself.

3. If I don't meet my personal goals, I will begin again and always forgive myself.

4. I will fight distraction and procrastination by figuring out what derails my work.

5. I will learn to feel good about myself without needing others' approval.

6. I'll reward myself when I meet my goals.

7. I'll find someone I can trust with whom I can share small successes (sibling, parent, aide, friend).

8. I won't get angry, because that doesn't make me a better writer or a better person.

Research note:

Creating a community of learners is an important initial step in making students feel safe in any learning situation. While teachers work to establish community—especially in writing workshop—early in the school year, it is important to monitor the community and repair it when there is a breach of confidence or when students fall into negative comments or attitudes. This is bound to happen, as we all are human. But helping students to remain positive and supportive of one another is critical. For an excellent study of this, read Ralph Peterson's book, *Life in a Crowded Place* (Heinemann, 1992).

The Struggling Writer

Garrett shares his plan with his teacher. She decides to make a plan for herself so she can support him. Below is her list with some revision; it includes some general ways that teachers can help students who dislike writing:

- Be professional in your reaction to the student, no matter what he or she says; negative emotions only fuel difficulty, so always react with kindness. You may have to watch yourself in the mirror to see the truth of how you react!

- Put yourself in the student's shoes; imagine how you would "walk out" of your difficulty. Talk to your student about this.

- Model courage in facing difficulty and patience with working through it.

- Focus on the process of getting better at something, not on the product a student produces.

- Minimize your anxiety about high-stakes testing, because you will communicate this to students; strugglers are anxious enough already.

- Work on your attitude; do not fall into grandstanding, shouting, or stand-offs.

- Build trusting relationships with students, based on kindness and unconditional love. This may take work, but it is worthwhile.

- Be steadfast, but with patience and gentleness. Do not accept procrastination, unless you've both agreed that the student, for example, will write after one drink of water and a walk around the room.

- Set up communication with home through e-mail or a sheet that travels back and forth. (See form at top of p. 16.)

- Understand that the student may not come to like writing, but he or she will still have strategies for doing it anyway.

My addition to the above list would be to post a quote from President Obama's inaugural address and read it aloud every day: ". . . there is nothing so satisfying to the spirit, so defining of our character than giving our all to a difficult task" (Obama, 2009). In fact, I'd list many "difficult tasks" and ask the students to spend the year inquiring into how thinkers overcome difficulty and figure out how to be successful. We all struggle with something,

Report to Parents

Use this form as a quick communication with parents about students' progress by checking the appropriate box in the third row and adding a short comment when appropriate.

Student:	Type of Writing:	Teacher:	Date:
4: student worked independently and thoroughly today	3: student mostly worked independently today and did class assignment	2: student tried to do work today, but was mostly unable to do it	1: student made little attempt to do work
Comment:	Comment:	Comment:	Comment:

whether or not we are honest about it. We can and will all succeed in some measure.

After several weeks, there is a marked change in Garrett's work and attitude toward writing. While there are still areas that need work, Garrett has developed the confidence to write for almost a page before he tires. When my time in his class is drawing to an end, he tells me that he "only hates writing a little now." Progress is slow. Still, Garrett knows that he can write when he has to, even though it may never be his favorite pastime.

Students Who Hate Writing Because All Writing Is Teacher-Focused

Most often, teachers who shun student-generated writing topics work in non-writing-workshop settings. This may be a school decision or the teacher's personal one, but it changes the way students view writing. Undoubtedly, one of the most joyful aspects of writing workshop is that students learn to trust themselves as thinker and writers. The joy of finding stories within one's own life and using them to communicate is freeing and empowering for young writers. However, in non-writing-workshop classes, teachers still

> I like videogames. My best game is final fantasy. I play it every day. I can beat my cousin and my uncle.
>
> After I play we go to get ice cream. Sometimes we get popcorn. I like to eat too.

Garrett tries to make writing bearable by writing about what he likes.

▲ Figure 1-1 *Garrett's writing sample*

hold the reins on assigning topics and on process. Clearly, there are some non-workshop teachers who do magnificent work, but students in these classrooms often misunderstand the purpose of writing, which is to communicate. Many of these students come to feel they are performing for the teacher, rather than learning to write from within and in any situation. This feeling can create a resistance that quickly grows into pure dislike.

There is no doubt that students must learn to respond to prompts (Angelillo, 2005b). Prompted writing is part of academic writing, high-stakes testing, and real-world situations. Nevertheless, prompted writing should not be the only type of writing students experience. If it is, students can easily become bored or lack engagement. Constantly responding to prompts teaches students—sometimes— to respond to prompts, but it does not teach them to be good writers. It is important to balance instruction with opportunities for students to write about topics and in genres of their choice.

> *Constantly responding to prompts teaches students—sometimes— to respond to prompts, but it does not teach them to be good writers.*

Of course, this raises the bar on teaching. It requires that the teacher be flexible and rigorous enough to understand that allowing students to self-select topics does not mean going haywire. It means finding ways to teach students to choose, develop, and angle a topic, and then to write about it well and with passion. And sometimes, it means saying "no." For example, a student may insist on writing about Alex Rodriguez, but this topic may not be appropriate for a letter to the president or a science report. Good writing instruction teaches students how to choose topics, how to angle them toward genre, and when to put a topic aside. So with respect to A-Rod, he won't be in a history report on the American Revolution, but he might be a good choice for a biography.

In the same school that Garrett attends, I visit another class where the teacher is teaching students to write nonfiction. The students have some choice about which topics to choose, but one student, Sarah, can't decide at all what to write about. In fact, when I sit with her for a conference, she puts her finger on her lips and rolls her eyes to the ceiling in the classic pose of "I haven't the vaguest idea what you want." This poor child is so confused. Here is a shortened version of our conference.

Teacher: How's it going?

Student: Fine. [She has written nothing on the page and doesn't even have a pencil.]

Teacher: Have you chosen your topic yet?

Student: Yep.

Teacher: Good! What is it?

Student: What?

Teacher: What's the topic?

Reasons for allowing students to choose their own topic in writing:

- When students choose their topics, the writing focus moves from the teacher to the students.

- They know more about topics they choose to write about.

- They tend to care about their writing when the topic has meaning to them.

- We can teach them more about writing itself when we are not "pulling teeth" to get them to write.

- We make them better writers—and thinkers—in the long run when we teach them to think deeply about an idea of their own.

The Struggling Writer

Student: [shrugs]

Teacher: Okay, let's talk about some ideas that are cooking in your head.

Student: [begins to tap fingers on desk] Well . . . umm . . .

The conference continues this way for another minute or so until I suggest to Sarah that she draw a quick sketch of something she would like to write about. She draws her baby sister. I ask her what she would like to say about her sister. Sarah looks at me long and whispers, "I don't know. Just tell me what you want me to write." Sarah may have other writing problems in addition to this, but foremost is her lack of understanding that writing belongs to her. She is leaning on me (or her teacher) to tell her what to do. How will she become an independent thinker? How will Sarah ever know what to write if someone doesn't tell her? She's become passive, unresponsive, and quiet. She's lost her voice, or, perhaps, she never had one. What do you do to help Sarah? We've all had Sarahs in our classes at one time or another, and often we just shake our heads in frustration or dismay. Despite the wonderful, respectful, and rigorous work that has been done in the last decades on improving writing instruction, some classrooms are still operating in a time warp of times past, times when we assigned a topic on Monday and expected a finished copy on Friday. Of these, some teachers would like to change, but they are terrified of "the test." So they fall back on methods that seem familiar, yet are not proven to work. For example, some teachers begin preparing for state writing tests on the first day of school. They assign topics from old tests. They hand out worksheets and drill, drill, drill. They enforce rigid formulas for numbers of sentences in each paragraph and numbers of paragraphs on a page. They "time" most writing assignments to teach students to write against the clock. These methods of themselves do not produce better scores, but under these conditions, the Sarahs in our classes become more passive, less confident, and eventually resistant. It is only by writing frequently and caring about writing that we get better at it. Please understand this: I am not advocating ignoring the test, nor do I think the tests are unimportant. However, I reiterate what I've written in other venues: Only rigorous writing in many genres for many audiences on topics of their choice will teach

> *It is only by writing frequently and caring about writing that we get better at it.*

How we can reach a child like Sarah:

• Introduce the "life story" concept to the student and help her hold on to it for most writing (see Chapter 2).

• Use drawing and oral storytelling to build confidence and supply details of the story.

• Coach the student through frequent conferring.

• Find a student partner who will encourage her while remaining focused on his own work.

• Break down writing assignments into smaller parts and walk through them with her.

• Help the student "see" the story potential in her life by pointing out stories that are embedded in her play with others, her conversations, her family events, and her accomplishments out of school.

• Encourage the student to use music, dance, or art to find ways to express her stories.

students to be excellent writers in any situation. Offering students only test-prep writing will make them stilted writers and narrow thinkers with little originality. They have little to say because they've not learned to write with passion. And they may not have good writing strategies for writing the little they can. Sadly, what they *do* learn is that someone else has to tell them what to think and write; we cannot abide this passivity in 21st-century education.

Only rigorous writing in many genres for many audiences on topics of their choice will teach students to be excellent writers in any situation.

I will not hammer away on this point. But I do encourage teachers who are frustrated about all their students "can't do" to look at their teaching. Balance your instruction between whole-group and individual teaching, between self-generating topics and assigned topics. Some students will whine that they have nothing to write. That's okay. They will figure it out, and their thinking skills will improve. Assigned topics had a purpose once upon a time, but the need for them as the sole way to spark writing died with the old factory schools. Let students learn to be problem solvers by finding writing topics in their own lives. It isn't easy or quick, but anything worthwhile rarely is.

Students Who Lack Essential Tools for Writing

While it is essential that all students have pens, pencils, or markers for writing, the tools to which I am referring are not this kind. The physical tools are easy to overcome: make sure supplies are provided and just move on, even if you need a monthly bake or fruit sale to do it. Never argue over broken pencil points, lost erasers, dry pens, and the like. Supplies can never become an excuse for not writing. Just say, "There are pencils in the box; there is paper on the shelf. Let's write."

However, students may lack other tools that are just as essential for writing, and not as easily provided. These tools are a writer's bank of knowledge: knowing how to make letters and making them with ease, understanding placement of words and sentences on the page, and having a solid foundation of spelling words and strategies to figure out new words. These are the "tools" students must have to write. And frankly, too many students are trying to write without them. It's as if we're trying to train athletes whom we've allowed to become grossly overweight because we don't want to bore them with fitness. What could be sillier?

I am not referring to emergent writers. We expect emergent writers to make their letters immaturely, use invented spelling, leave out words they can't spell, and so on. But this is a stage they must outgrow. A fifth grader who still can't spell *went* or distinguish between when to use upper- and lowercase letters can feel seriously challenged when it's time to write an essay. Here are some suggestions for setting goals in middle and upper grades to change this:

- Please do not tell your students that spelling doesn't count—because it does. Period.

- Do not tell students they can add in the punctuation later. Punctuation is a unit of composition, not something writers sprinkle on at the end.

- Find time in your day to teach word skills, affixes, root words, irregular verbs, verb tenses, letter formation, and so on. Obviously, you can't teach this all in one day and get anything else done. But do not ignore it. Most students will not just pick it up.

- Find a thoughtful and thorough spelling guide, such as Sandra Wilde's *Spelling Strategies and Patterns* (2007) or Diane Snowball and Faye Bolton's *Spelling K–8* (1999), and use it every day with humor and a smile, noting how much students can do or approximate, not what they lack.

At the risk of raising the ire of many, I also suggest that we reinstate some kind of minimal handwriting practice. No, I am not recommending a return to the 1950s, when we practiced handwriting for hours until our fingers swelled. The expectation at that time was that we'd be handwriting letters and reports, so a beautiful handwriting style was desirable. Now most of us word-process our work or we use text-messaging and e-mail. These are modes of communication Miss Dunne would never have predicted—or allowed—when I was in third grade. Oh, the perfection she required of the capital *Q*! How harshly we were judged by the lowercase *p*! What pain she inflicted on little hands that could not hold the pen the "proper" way! My fingers ache at the thought.

And yet . . . and yet . . . until we can obtain laptop computers for all our students— and I hope this will happen in the near future—they must be able to write so that they, and their teachers, can read it. For students who cannot make their letters because of hand discomfort or other issues, let's teach them to type immediately. I don't mean the hunt-and-peck typing that so many of us know. I mean the real deal, including building speed and accuracy. How about a 10-week after-school course on word processing for students? We do this for test prep—let's do it for writing.

In one classroom I know, the teacher was so concerned about how handwriting impedes student writing progress that he decided to work on it. Al teaches fourth grade, and five of his students—including one or two potentially super writers—just couldn't get their writing done because their handwriting slowed them down so much. Al established a writing corner, where students who needed extra support in *anything* could go for practice. Initially, he developed three modules for study (handwriting, spelling, conventions), with plans to add others later on. Then, through conferring, he asked students to agree to work on one module for three weeks. Thus, on any day, one student was working on handwriting with a partner, while two others were working on a spelling study. Al collected pre-corner samples and post-corner samples of writing (see Figure 1-2), and afterward determined that the work helped build both skill and confidence. Giving students time to concentrate on background work they needed to make writing easier was well worth the time.

Spelling: Students worked independently to correct spelling in one or two sentences. At this point, they were responsible for working toward accuracy not perfection.

Francis Oct. 3 Wen I go to the prak I pla bazbol wit my bruder.	Francis Oct. 9 _Wen_ I go to the _prak_ I pla _bazbol_ wit my bruder.
Jenisia Nov. 1 I tack dancing lesons. I wer soft tites and bala shoos.	Jenisia Nov. 4 I take dancing lesons. I wear soft tigts and ballet shoes.
Paulette Jan. 19 My dog had pupys and they are cute. I whant to kepe them but my mother says no.	Paulette Jan. 21 My dog had puppies and they are cute. I want to kepp them but my mother said no.

Conventions: Students studied a simple mentor text independently and attempted to adjust conventions according to what the mentor author did.

Joshua September 18 my sister was born when I was two and she is taller now than me and I wish I would grow like her	Joshua September 20 My sister was born when I was two. She is taller than me now. I wish I would grow.
Emmy Nov. 22 Today is my birthday and I will have my party on Saturday at chuckiecheez and my friends will come but not my cousins because they are too young	Emmy Nov. 23 Today is my birthday! I will have my party on Saturday at...Chuck e cheese! My friends will come, but not my cousins. They are too young!

▲ Figure 1-2 _Grade 4 students' work on basics in independent modules_

- Set aside a corner for practice. Try to find a small round table and make the corner as comfortable as possible; if possible, provide a nourishing snack (fruit) and/or soft music to make corner work as positive as possible.

- Inform students that all of them will have a rotation in the corner for some type of practice; this will make it not seem like punishment.

- Develop activities that directly support handwriting (see below).

- Post names of students assigned to corner activities by week; these students spend 10–15 minutes of writing time in the practice corner.

- Provide activities that include some of the following: tracing letters with a finger on light sandpaper; drawing letters with water onto paper with a wet finger; tracing over letters from one page of a Big Book; half-page of letter practice; writing one line from independent reading book in best writing; doing an oral or written reflection on how handwriting is improving and what else student needs to do; posting improved handwriting from notebooks; doing partner work to discuss procedure for making letters.

Figure 1-3 *Teacher's list of ideas for setting up corner activities that support handwriting*

Summary

Teachers hope that students will come to school filled with excitement and the desire to write. We know this happens much of the time, but there are certainly a number of students for whom writing is unpleasant. For these students, it is important that we teach self-monitoring plans and making goals for writing. If we think of the challenges we all carry in our personal lives (see Figure 1-4 on p. 26), we develop not only compassion for students who dislike writing but also strategies to work through the difficulty.

Activities to promote independent handwriting practice

• Student traces letters on printed page with finger, then with marker.

• Student circles letters on printed page that fall below the line; then student traces them.

• Student chooses one letter he writes well and one he doesn't and draws them all over a one-quarter sheet of paper.

• Student practices letters with different writing implements: gel pens, markers, highlighters, thick and thin pencils (crayons do not produce crisp letters, so do not offer them).

• Student decides which implement is most comfortable for his hands and uses that for most writing.

• Students read a partner's writing and then coach each other about how to make letters that are difficult for readers to discern.

• Student practices letters by writing them large, then very small, fast, then slow, the way musicians practice difficult passages of music.

• Student self-assesses to determine which part of his handwriting needs his attention next.

To-do list for teachers:

⁕ Think honestly about the degree to which you are comfortable with self-selected topics and consider moving in that direction, if needed.

⁕ Work on establishing a safe community by modeling kind responses, respectful requests, and acceptance of approximation of learning.

⁕ Gather your most resistant writers into a small group and ask them to talk about what is hard for them about writing; tape their conversation and use it to plan your teaching.

⁕ Make sure you ask students to do only one thing at a time!

- How do you feel when you have to write something?

- What do you do about it? Do you procrastinate?

- How do you decide on the genre, and how does that help you?

- How do you get your ideas?

- How does the planning stage help you? What could you do to have it help you more?

- How do you get a draft down? Then what do you do?

- How do you react to length requirements or no stated length?

- How do you know you are done?

- What do you do to revise?

- How do you use conventions to shape meaning?

- How do you get ready to publish?

- How do you use a mentor text to help you?

- Role-play each of the types of struggling writers: What does the student say? How does the compassionate and wise teacher respond?

Figure 1-4 *Imagine yourself as a struggling writer . . .*

The Struggling Writer

2

"I have nothing to say"

Struggling to Find, Trust, and Develop Ideas

Early in my daughter's year in second grade, her teacher sent home a note requesting a conference. With a pain in the pit of my stomach, I visited the teacher after school the next day.

"I'm afraid she isn't listening in class," the teacher said with annoyance. "She doesn't raise her hand, and when I call on her, she has nothing to say."

Hmm, that description sounded nothing like the chatterbox I knew at home. And the "not listening in class" part sounded fishy to me, because Cheryl was quite good at eavesdropping on all sorts of conversations. I was confused.

After dinner that evening, I gently spoke to Cheryl: "Mrs. X says you don't raise your hand and you have nothing to say in class."

Cheryl giggled. "I have lots to *think*, but I have nothing to *say* . . . to her." Ah. Now it was clear. Cheryl had not learned that what you think becomes what you say, and what you say becomes what you write. The thinking-talking-writing connection had not clicked for my daughter.

To be fair to Cheryl, I don't think this connection was being taught in her classroom. The class was definitely a "fill in the worksheet" kind of place. No wonder Cheryl had little to say—if there is no negotiation of meaning and no value on what is going on in children's heads (other than finding the right answers to the teacher's questions), inquisitive little minds may tune out. Note that I did not say "turn off." Very few minds turn off; they just redirect themselves to other interests: Why does dust shine in the sunlight? Why is that dog sniffling at the classroom window? Who invented magic markers? Why do stomachs grumble? If I were a princess . . . . There is lots going on in those little heads, but students think little of it applies to their teachers' demands.

In this chapter, we will look at one major difficulty of strugglers, especially in writing workshop classrooms: finding self-selected topics. As I have indicated elsewhere, I do not recommend routinely giving teacher-generated topics to students. Certainly, assigning topics *appears* to be easier for all: At least students have something to gnaw on and won't whine as much. But in the end, this only teaches them that we do not believe they have ideas worth writing about. Furthermore, it says we don't value their thinking or, at its extreme, that we believe they can't think. To my mind, this is just not worth the expedience of the moment. Long-term teaching is about thinking and writing across years and for whole lives. In this chapter, we'll help students who struggle with ideas find confidence and support as thinkers and writers by doing the following exercises:

- Generating a bank of ideas
- Using talking and sketching as ways to write
- Finding and working on a "life story"

Generating a Bank of Ideas

One of the strongest arguments for writing workshop is the way it teaches students to search within themselves for a topic. Obviously, teachers offer assistance through modeling and conferring, but the emphasis remains on what is important to the students in terms of topics. This is critical, because if students care about their topics, they will be inclined to want to write well about them. If students do not care, they'll expend as little effort as possible. If we can get students to care about their topics, then we can teach them strategies for becoming better writers.

When Miss Dunne assigned my 1950s third-grade class to write about the opening of the Throgs Neck Bridge in the Bronx, I was numb with boredom. I remember writing very little and earning a fat, red C. Ah, if only she'd asked me to write about what was on my mind: my grandmother dying, my best friend moving away, the argument I had with my cousin, what I didn't get for Christmas, that spinach gives me bellyaches, how my Sunday dress itched . . . at least I could have filled up the page!

The first order of business for all students in writing workshop, and most gingerly and respectfully for the strugglers, is teaching them that their minds are full of ideas. I often challenge students to try to *not* think for 30 seconds, and, of course, they can't do it. The work is to transfer those thoughts into ideas students will recognize as worthy for the page.

> *The first order of business for all students in writing workshop, and most gingerly and respectfully for the strugglers, is teaching them that their minds are full of ideas.*

Shaking Up Our Thinking

For years we have been teaching young writers to keep writer's notebooks. This is still an excellent practice, but teachers sometimes use these notebooks in ways that make me nervous. As a writer, I do not force myself to write at least a page every night. I do something to feed my writing life every day, but notebook entries may not be what I need. For example, I may be trying to generate ideas for a speech I need to write. In this case, my notebook will be filled notes and quotes, fragments and little tidbits of thoughts. Or I may be writing a poem for my husband's birthday. Weeks ahead, I'd be collecting words I might use, as well as playing with the sounds of words together. All this may seem too sophisticated for students, but it isn't. It's about purpose. Their notebooks must be real or their interest will wane.

As for notebooks being real, I suggest that we move away from the "everyone decorates a black-and-white marbled notebook" way of thinking. For our strugglers, even the length of one page of those notebooks is daunting. Why not let some students try using a small memo pad? My son, for example, carries a memo pad in the pocket of his cargo pants. Why not allow some students to choose that kind of notebook? And this does not mean only strugglers; anyone might decide to use a memo pad, sketch pad, or whatever. It's a matter of choice. If we want them to make choices, we have to allow and respect their choices.

Here are some choices for keeping notebooks that may be less intimidating for some writers:

• Small journal

• Small memo pad or steno pad

• Collection of index cards (with some way to hold them together)

• A computer notebook kept on a disc

• A sketch pad or book without lines

• Speaking into a program that transcribes speech onto the computer

• Several sheets of paper stapled together for keeping notes on one particular project

The Struggling Writer

So how does this approach affect generating ideas? As thinkers, we are always generating ideas, but often students do not recognize them as such. Sometimes they have an idea, and their biggest worry is whether or not it will be accepted by the teacher. In the last chapter, we met Sarah, who stared at the ceiling when I asked her a question. I am quite sure that she was not thinking, "Nothing's going on in this brain," but rather, "What on earth does this teacher want me to say?" She wanted so much to please me that she was frozen. It was better to say nothing—and have me fill in the blanks for her—than to get it wrong. Students often learn that if they sit long enough without answering, we will give them the answer! Teachers are uncomfortable with silence. One of my mentors, Carl Anderson, taught me to wait—and it was the hardest thing to do. Try waiting when a student doesn't respond immediately. It's hard to do but, as Carl taught me, students usually say something eventually, and we can begin to teach from that point on.

Idea Generation

Any book on writing workshop will contain strategies for getting students to generate ideas. I suggest you read some of them if they are not already part of your professional library. (See list of recommended books on page 55.) However, we also note that for many strugglers, these strategies don't seem to work. How can this be? We know there are lots of ideas in their minds. What's keeping them from letting those ideas pour out?

Let's assume for a moment that some students have difficulty putting their ideas in a container. That is, their ideas float by, but they have trouble separating them, or speaking about them in concrete and specific ways. So a thought such as "my baby sister" does not yield more thinking for them because they don't know how to separate "baby sister" into a series of discrete events or attributes. The most they say is "I love her" or "She's cute." All the many events surrounding the baby sister are lost in a blur.

The concept of self-monitoring can be applied here. We think of self-monitoring as lists of ways to get started and keep going, of setting goals, of finding conditions for learning that meet a student's needs. Self-monitoring should also include "ways to stretch thinking." The student who cannot get beyond "my baby sister" needs specific strategies

Why some students won't let us in on their thinking:

• They are unsure about exactly what we mean by "thoughts"!

• They don't think their thoughts are important.

• They are embarrassed about what they are thinking or they want to keep it private.

• They cannot imagine how their thoughts can fit into a school setting.

• They are anxious or nervous about something unrelated to writing workshop.

• They have not learned to trust us yet.

• Their past experience in school has taught them that it is too dangerous to let the teacher know what you are thinking.

• All their thoughts mesh together into a blur.

• They are afraid of saying something we will judge as "wrong."

• They hope we will tell them exactly what they should say in response to our questions.

to go deeper into the idea. In some ways, this is extrapolation, and in other ways, it is just teaching students ways to access what is already hiding in their minds and teaching them to use these strategies on their own.

Sarah is this kind of student. We met her in Chapter 1, when she struggled to figure out how I wanted her to respond. Let's go back to her. As I work with Sarah over several

Ways to stretch thinking about a simple idea:

• Draw about it.

• Make it into a song or fit it into a familiar tune.

• Use a repeated phrase to tell the story.

• Add what you thought or felt.

• Expand how you feel about it.

• Explain why it is part of your life.

weeks, I know she needs encouragement and support. But she also needs to become fairly independent, since neither I nor her teacher will be there to coach her forever on every piece of writing. It would seem easy to give Sarah a list of ideas and then let her work on it, but I decide that in her case, less is more. I would rather she know how to work well with two or three strategies than 10 strategies that leave her overwhelmed and confused. Ultimately, I want Sarah to think globally, but for now, I want her to learn to trust her thinking.

> *I would rather she know how to work well with two or three strategies rather than 10 strategies that leave her overwhelmed and confused.*

I begin by telling her that I'm going to teach her two ways to get herself to talk and write about her sister. Each way is a specific strategy that she can use with the "my baby sister" topic, but my plan is that she will use the strategies to help her with other writing.

The first strategy is to think of a color that goes with the topic. Sarah smiles and says, "Pink!"

"Okay," I answer. "Tell me what's pink about your sister."

Sarah thinks. "Well, her room is pink . . . and she has a pink coat."

"Stop!" I say. "Let's write that down."

Sarah writes *room* and *coat* under the word *pink* on a quarter sheet of paper. Then I tell her I must confer with another student, so her work is to spend five minutes thinking of one other pink item to add to her baby sister list.

When I return, Sarah has added *blanket* and *hat* to the list. She tells me she can think of two more things to add—*stuffed bunny* and *binkie*. I conclude she's gotten the idea, so I tell her that color is something that can always help her to say more about any topic. We practice aloud for a minute with my topic: my dog. Sarah says the color black, and we add *fur*, *collar*, and *leash* to my list. Then I leave Sarah to go back to her idea and to write an entry about her sister and the color pink.

When we meet again, I suggest to Sarah that another way to say more about her topic is to think about *firsts*. I explain that *firsts* means the first time something happened or that she noticed something. She returns to the topic of her baby sister and writes *firsts* at the top of a quarter sheet of paper. She asks, "You mean like the first time I got to see her?" I nod. Sarah writes that on the list, then, over the course of the next five minutes, she adds, "first tooth, the first time she got a cold, first Christmas." I explain to Sarah that each of these items on her list is a little story. By envisioning the event, she can use each first and make it into a story. Sarah is relieved to have her own list. More important, she has two ways that she can make any one idea into longer writing. (See Figure 2-1, pages 35–36.)

It is critical to remember that learning is a process. Sometimes we hand students lists of ways to do something and expect them to perform. For someone like Sarah, it is better to have two strategies she has practiced and had success with than a list of 20 strategies that freeze her in her tracks. It is better to teach less. Teach only one thing at a time. Teach it thoroughly. Allow time for practice. Build on it slowly. Have lists in your back pocket (see Figure 2-2, What a Teacher Can Do to Help Students Generate Ideas for Writing, page 37) but resist handing them out without careful modeling and demonstration (see Figures 2-3, page 38, and 2-4, page 39).

Something to Think About

I write this with caution and in a spirit of love and respect: I wonder to what degree some teachers do not respect the topics their struggling students choose. To what degree do we find ourselves saying, "Can't you write about something better?" Do we struggle with ways to teach students to write about topics we think are boring? How judgmental are we toward these students? When we are tired or stressed, it is easy to lose the gentle compassion we may ordinarily have for strugglers. It is those times when we can damage a student's efforts at writing. Struggling writers require our most professional, generous, and deliberate efforts to understand and provide support.

Figure 2-1 *Ideas for expanding self-selected topics into longer writing: Use as ways to generate thinking and writing about a topic (teach one at a time)*

• Color, shape, smell, texture

• Firsts, lasts, every day, once

• What is good, bad, angry, mean, kind, or gentle about it (or a time that this happened)?

• What is happy about it? Sad? What makes you laugh? Cry?

• Is there a secret hidden in it? A funny story?

• What are your unique thoughts about it?

My topic: *my dog*	Expanding my thinking
color	She's black
shape	Dog shape! Very big!
smell	Warm dog, wet dog, dirty dog . . .
texture	Bumpy, rough, or smooth fur
firsts	First time I had a dog for a long time
lasts	Last time I went to visit my dad she was with me
every day	We go for a walk
once	She ran away
good	She is always happy to see me
bad	She makes messes on the floor
mean	She chases squirrels
kind	She keeps my feet warm
gentle	She lets the cats sleep curled up with her
happy	She loves me

(continued on page 36)

sad	She's getting old
secret	I spend too much money on her
funny story	When she broke into my neighbor's house and sat on the couch and ate candy
makes you cry	When she walks into trees because she is blind
unique	She knows when I am coming home before I get there!

A third-grade teacher told me recently that one of her boys—who "has potential"—was wasting it because he would only write about wrestling. I talked to the student, and he had a vast knowledge of wrestling moves and rivalries, as well as the history of wrestling. Not my cup of tea but, nevertheless, impressive. Alas, those of us who do not follow the melodrama of wrestling entertainment can certainly perceive this topic as boring or nonacademic. But those folks who enjoy wrestling might not like coming to the opera with me. If I chose to write about the opera every day, would you tell me to change my topic? Hmm . . . probably not, because I would be writing about something more "acceptable." In fact, you might think I was practicing to be a critic. So for those youngsters who insist on writing about wrestling, or dirt biking, or skateboarding, or monsters and aliens . . . let them do it! Let them be critics! And teach them something good about writing while they are engaged in topics that matter to them.

I can hear your objections: But they have to learn to write about something else! They can't write about aliens forever! And what will they do on the test? Yes, you are all correct. They need to do all these things. But not now. Not until they learn something about writing and about trusting themselves with another topic. Eventually, they will learn about audience and about voice. Eventually, they will turn their attention to something

- Think aloud about his/her process for getting ideas.

- Teach students to talk aloud about thought processes and possible ideas; teach how to decide whether to keep or discard them.

- Teach students to keep a writer's notebook, memo pad, computer file, or folder for collecting ideas.

- Teach students to become metacognitive. (i.e., aware of their own thinking process)

- Work on specific strategies for getting ideas (see next section below).

- Build student confidence and trust in their ideas.

- Avoid being judgmental.

- Work on idea lists early in the year and all year long.

- Scaffold the concept of a "life story" idea (see section beginning on page 41).

Figure 2-2 *What a teacher can do to help students generate ideas for writing*

else—baseball, lunar landings, *American Idol*. Someday they will abandon the aliens and wrestling, and at that point, they need to know *how to write*. We may not see them abandon those topics while they are in our classes, but we are confident that we are sowing good writing seeds. We trust they will be good writers when they come out from under the "only one topic" spell.

Using Talking and Sketching as Ways to Write

We teach primary students to draw as a window into writing, but we abandon this practice too soon. Many students in later grades might find that drawing or sketching is

- Notice what floats through your mind and name it (the moon, what I have to do next, my hand hurts, my sister, cleaning my room, a song I can't forget, the smell of onions, it's too dark . . .).
- Name what you see, hear, or smell (I see my mother cooking, I hear the chicken crackling in the frying pan, I smell the fried chicken).
- Notice your feelings, including what they feel like (e.g., I feel tired, and it makes my body feel like I'm melting into the chair).
- Think about what worries you or makes you happy (I worry about bullies, I am happy playing with my cousin).
- Think about what you love, like, dislike (I love my dog, I like walking her, I dislike cleaning up after her).
- Think about what you want to do or don't want to do (I want to go out to play, I don't want to make my bed in the morning).
- Notice what surprises you (I didn't know my brother gets mad when I whistle).
- Notice changes in your everyday world (today there was a dead mouse on the sidewalk).
- Notice what remains the same (every night my dad watches baseball).
- Name what galls you (my brother takes my baseball glove without asking, my cousin doesn't have to eat his vegetables).
- Consider what inspires you (watching basketball on TV).
- Identify what makes you feel weary (too much homework, going shopping with my mother).
- Think about what you do often (tease my cousin).
- Think about what or whom you miss (I miss my grandma).
- Work on idea lists early in the year and all year.
- Scaffold the concept of a "life story" idea (see page 41).

Figure 2-3 *Specific strategies for getting ideas that teachers can model*

The Struggling Writer

- From just being alive and learning how to "see" into life

- Books

- Everyday living (schoolyard, bus ride, home routines)

- Friendships and other relationships (bullies, someone you see every day but don't know, adults in your life)

- Family (relationships, routines, disruptions, conflict)

- Environment (what's in your house, room, neighborhood, on the route to school, church, soccer practice)

- Content area information (what intrigues you about science, social studies, or math?)

- Personal interests

- Games, sports, video games, TV, movies, etc.

- Recollections (anything that happened before right now)

- Special days and what makes them different (no one came to my birthday party, it was too cold for a cookout on July 4th)

- Surprises (birds in winter! mouse in the bathtub! baby brother climbed out of crib! my hair got long!)

- Ordinary things (cupcakes, bus fumes, fire hydrants, braids, radios, car horns, dirty diapers)

- Everyday smells (coffee, baby's skin, pipe smoke, cut grass, mother's powder)

- Everyday sounds (baby crying, car brakes, motorcycles, planes overhead, school bell, a neighbor laughing)

- Smells in special places (grandmother's house, church candles, nurse's office, cafeteria, deli, hospital, library)

- Things you think are bad (my haircut is ugly, I think my cousin started smoking, there is garbage in the street, the elevator is broken, peanut butter is sticky)

Figure 2-4 *Noticing: Where do writers get their ideas?*

a useful way to get and develop ideas. In our desire for students to write more, usually in preparation for state writing tests, we eliminate this step in the thinking process. For some students, making a full-fledged drawing can help them access ideas and details. For others, a small sketch will do. Yet others might benefit from some kind of visual representation of their thinking. Teachers like to point students toward "graphic organizers," but often a visual of the student's own creation is enough to make thinking flow.

In Al's fourth-grade room, I work with Kathy, a struggling writer, to demonstrate that as I tell my story aloud, my sketches—silly as they are—help me remember what I want to write. I tell Kathy the story of my morning:

"I woke up this morning and I was late!" (I draw a stick figure of myself with wild morning hair next to a bed). "So I got dressed quickly, but I couldn't find my socks." (I draw two socks.) "I looked in the laundry basket." (I draw a basket.) "I looked in my sneakers." (I draw sneakers.) "Finally, I looked under the bed. There they were! My cat had stolen them and was asleep on top of them." (I draw a cat sleeping.)

I tell Kathy that now I have the sketches, I can remember the story and go back to write it. In fact, Kathy "reads" my story back to me as I point to my sketches. Then Kathy tells me the story of going to the park with her aunt. As she talks, I draw sketches to capture each part of the story for her. She looks them over and corrects them. "I have braids, not short hair," she says. So when Kathy is not trying to hold both the story and the task of writing in her head, she is able to recall and correct the details of her story.

Teachers might also consider that, for strugglers, the sketches can be credited as "writing," at least until the students find their voices. In its widest definition, writing includes all modes of written communication. I suggest that we allow students more opportunity to use drawing and sketching as ways to compose. I know there is the concern that students must write and practice writing. Yes, this is true. But if students are resistant or unable to write, it is better to break the ice with sketching than to have no writing at all.

Finding and Working on a "Life Story"

Everyone has a story. It's the story that is on our minds most of the time, the one we want to write about most often. It may be about a great tragedy or joy in life. It may be about a good friendship or the breakup of a bad one. Adults usually have two or three great narratives in their lives: the birth of a child, a divorce, the championship college game, wartime experiences, the faithful pet, and so on. In fact, Donald Murray once said that for our whole lives we only really write about one or two things. Of course, as adults, we may write to explore a theme: loneliness, betrayal, faith and hope, courage. Young writers usually write about an actual story, something that looms large in their minds. This is good and deep for them. It yields good writing, if allowed to grow and be nurtured. So it is sad that many teachers say, "Don't tell me you're writing about your dog again! Find something else to write about today!" How can they write from their hearts when we force them to lie about what matters to them?

When I was in sixth grade, President Kennedy was assassinated. Just as with many of my generation, I remember exactly where I was and what I was doing when I found out. For days we were saturated via television with the Dallas motorcade, the mournful funeral, the investigation, the murder of Oswald, and consequences of those events. Years later, a high school teacher clued me into something: She said that no matter what someone asks you to write about, you can always relate it to Kennedy's assassination. It was true. On college applications, test prompts, and later job application essays, I could write about the many ways my life was affected by that day. In fact, I discovered that I could answer almost any question through the lens of that one tragic event.

We can adapt this idea for young writers by teaching them that they each have at least one life story. I emphasize that it does not have to be a tragic global event, like the Kennedy assassination. For youngsters, it may be something as simple as their pets. Fine, let them write about Fido. But teach them to deepen their thinking about Fido, to look at Fido through different lenses, to play with words and humor, to think about dogs in general. In short, let them become experts on their topics.

I recall one young, reluctant writer who cared for little else but fishing. He could talk about tides, lines, bait, lures, and other things I care nothing about. He was passionate about this one thing. We took his aversion to writing and turned it into something positive. He worked all year on his "Fishing Chronicles," because we gave him permission to write about fishing as much as he wanted. From there, he eventually wrote memoirs about fishing with his grandfather, nonfiction about types of fish, persuasive essays about stopping pollution that kills fish, and so on. His writing did not become stellar overnight, but at least he produced writing that mattered to him and that was academically appropriate.

Again, I hear the objections already: "He has to learn to write about other things!" "What if the test doesn't have anything about fishing on it?" and so on. All true, but this bears emphasizing. What if our young writer won't write at all? That won't help him become a better writer, will it? With his life story, he is able to learn to see a topic from different perspectives, in varying genres, and, because of his passion for the topic, to work on qualities of good writing (Culham, 2003). Each time we force a struggling student to take on a new topic, we pull the rug out from under him. He is comfortable with fishing, or dogs, or frogs, or baseball, or his baby sister, or his grandfather . . . and we take that comfort away and expect him to perform. It doesn't make sense, and it surely is not humane.

Talk with your strugglers about their lives in conferences. Find out what they care deeply about. Ask their parents, if you have to. Use this information to build their confidence. Remember that it must be something they know well and can talk about a lot! Over the last few years, here are some life stories students have shared with me:

- A relationship with a grandfather or grandmother

- An uncle or aunt (often away in another state or in the armed forces)

- A pet (and some very unusual ones!)

- A sister, brother, cousin, or parent

- A best friend

The Struggling Writer

- Baseball, football, skateboarding, basketball, hockey

- Magic tricks

- Fishing, skiing, ice fishing, snowboarding, hunting, hiking, camping, swimming

- Building model ships and planes

- Train sets

- Wrestling

- Movies

- Professional sports (Yankees, Red Sox, Giants, Jets, ESPN, the Super Bowl)

- Playing in the park

- Local amusement parks, Disney World, the circus

- Video games, iPods, iPhones, handheld games

- Cooking/baking

- Juggling

I heard the groans out there when you read *video games*! Alas, these games are here to stay, for a while at least. I agree that it is hard to write well about video games because students tend to write about how they play a game. (*And then I got to the next level, and I killed two aliens, and I got to the next level, and . . . .*) This is as interesting as watching 500 slides of someone else's vacation. However, if this is what they care about, then our work is to teach them to write well about it. Remember that sketching and listing are two ways to help students write. Ask video gamers to use sketches to write about their games, and to use one of the ideas from Figure 2-1 to help them expand their thinking. For example, if a gamer is writing about a particular game and using "color," she might be led to write that orange lights always mean the enemy is sneaking around the corner, and the "good guys" are always dressed in yellow. This is far better than merely telling us about how yesterday's game went.

One of the benefits of writing about a life story is the momentum it builds. Students live these real stories in their lives outside of school, so every moment can be preparation for writing. Everything they do that relates to their life passion becomes writing material. I demonstrate this by sharing my life story, or at least the one that is most school-appropriate. The life story I share is the unending shenanigans of my dogs. They do something every day that is fodder for writing, and I show that I am collecting ideas from them constantly. I don't have to really work at this; it just happens because I spend time with the dogs every day. In fact, when I return to classes week after week, one of the first questions students ask me is, "How are Java and Ruby? What did they do this week?" They are interested because the depth and breadth of my story has hooked them.

Just using the antics of the dogs, I have written numerous lists of ideas, collected words I want to use, and composed notebook entries, persuasive essays, reports on dogs, letters to authorities, fictional stories based on reality, memoirs, poetry, and a few silly songs. Each of these is a model for students of how to "work" an idea and mine it for the most they can. It's not enough to say over and over that "I love my dogs." I have to use that love to get myself going with lots of thinking and writing. And I can do this because I know the dogs so well.

On the following page Figure 2-5 lists ways to take a life story and build it into more writing: Use a similar list to help your students begin to see the limitless possibilities of staying and working with one good idea.

Summary

We've seen that most students who feel they have nothing to say usually have lots going on but don't know how to translate that into writing. Using techniques such as talking, sketching, and staying with one story for a long time, we can build confidence in these writers. Once students know that their ideas are worthwhile and are expandable, they are ready to learn strategies for turning their ideas into longer writing projects.

Life-story thinking	How it translates into writing
Write about a past event or memory related to the life story.	I remember the day I brought Ruby home. I remember the first time Java stole Ruby's food. I remember the time they broke into my neighbor's house. I remember all the baby bunnies they've brought to me as gifts.
Write about what you are thinking right now about the life story.	When I am in school, I really miss them. I am worried about Ruby because she is sick. I hope Java didn't knock down the Christmas tree again. When I get home, I want to take them for a run. I have to check if they need shots; oops, they need food!
Write down words that describe your life story.	Exciting, busy, exhausting, funny, silly, smelly
Write down something bad that happened.	Java pulled me to chase a squirrel and I broke my hand. Java bit a puppy. Ruby and Java fight over treats. Java ran away. Ruby ate the monthly bills.
Write what you like best about it.	I like to sleep on the floor between them. I like the way they smell. I like that they always love to play with me. I like that they are always happy to see me. I like that they are strong and big.

Figure 2-5 Ways to take a life story and build it into more writing

To-do list for teachers:

- Practice listening to students without giving them the answers you want to hear.

- Resolve to be open-minded about students' selection of topics.

- Focus on teaching qualities of good writing, regardless of the topic.

- Develop the concept of the "life story" in your classroom.

- Find and use your own life story as a teaching tool for modeling thinking and writing.

3

"I'm done!"

Struggling to Build Stamina, Manage Time, and Focus on Writing Work

My mother was an immaculate homemaker. Windows washed, bathrooms spotless, floors clean enough to eat on—you get the picture. It's not surprising that she expected her daughters to help her keep everything in order. I recall one time my sister and I were charged with folding clean laundry Mommy had taken off the clothesline (dryers weren't the commonplace household item they are now). We folded a few towels, threw a few washcloths at each other, and ended up chasing each other through the house. To Mommy's query about the laundry, we shouted, "We're done!" We ran outside, off to play tag or jump rope. Of course, there were still piles of unfolded laundry on the bed, but our attention was elsewhere. We were, indeed, done. We were on to the next exercise in merriment. Mommy wasn't pleased.

When I think back on this situation, I realize that it is analogous to writing. For example, my sister and I did not think that the laundry was directly connected to us. It was *Mommy's* issue. We really didn't care, not because we were bad kids but just because we were *kids*. If Mommy insisted that the clothes be folded neatly and put away, that need belonged to her. We were just as happy taking wrinkled clothes right out of the laundry basket to wear. (We probably would have been happy wearing dirty clothes if it meant we didn't have to fold them!)

Some young students feel the same way about writing. They do not see that writing is in any way connected to them or relevant to their lives. It is the *teacher's* issue. They are just being kids, getting through the task with as little effort as possible before something else grabs their attention and sends them off in another direction. In fact, to their thinking, writing may keep them from having fun—like those piles of laundry kept my sister and me from running outside to the playground. So they figure out how to do as little as possible, which provides time for other pursuits, like roaming the room, drinking water, going to the bathroom, or digging in the desk.

We need to consider how to teach students to just keep going, to have the stick-to-itiveness to do and write more. It is "in the doing of it" that the most learning occurs, not in the completing of a task. Students who do little cheat themselves of learning, of experience, and of developing a habit of being that will help them throughout life. Ruth Sidney Charney (2002) tells us, "Children—and adults—mistake ease of learning for the overall potential to learn. They confuse speed with facility. . . . We need to show respect for the doing as well as the done, and for the slow and steady rate of acquisition. . . . The willingness to sustain effort and the courage to persist may be as important to achievement as any teaching methodology" (p. 378).

> *Students who do little cheat themselves of learning, of experience, and of developing a habit of being that will help them throughout life.*

The Struggling Writer

In this chapter, we'll look at these types of writers and ways to help them build stamina for writing. We'll look at issues of time and amount, as well as strategies for helping students to stick with a writing project for longer periods of time. We'll look at the following:

- Teaching ownership and pride in writing

- Strategies for elaboration

- Stretching students' stamina for writing

Teaching Ownership and Pride in Writing

This is the challenging part of this work, because we're attempting to teach students to care about writing, when they see little use in it. We are trying to overcome some immature student attitudes, such as "How can I care about writing . . ."

- when it belongs to the teacher because he cares about it and I don't?

- when the teacher makes me do it over anyway?

- when the more I write, the more I have to "fix"?

- when the teacher always tells me to go back and reread it?

- when my spelling and conventions make it hard to read?

- when my handwriting makes it hard to read?

So many students are defeated before they begin.

We have little need to defend writing instruction—there is a body of evidence for the efficacy of writing instruction that is continents long—but we do need to communicate better with students. This does not mean lectures about how writing will help them get good jobs one day. Most eight-year-olds are not thinking about life in 10 years. But writing that is entertaining, therapeutic, and informative may be worthwhile, in their estimation.

Annie is a fourth grader who finishes her work in minutes. She all but shouts, "I'm done!" before we see her chatting with students at another table and eating cookies she's hidden in her desk. Her teacher asks to see her writing, and Annie proudly brings it over. Of course, we predict correctly that she's only written a few words. (See Figure 3-3 on page 54 for progression of Annie's writing.)

"Is this your whole story?" I ask, looking at the few lines on the paper.

She looks at me as if I'm crazy. "Yep, that's it."

I ask her to tell me more about her story. "I told you, that's it," she says.

There are many strategies for writing more that I can teach Annie, but at this time, it is more important to teach Annie to care about her writing. (Look for the strategies later in this chapter.) Annie clearly doesn't care. Writing—to Annie—belongs to her teacher. The assignment belongs to her teacher. Annie does it minimally, to placate her teacher, but her heart is not in it.

Caring is a major ingredient for success in most endeavors. Whether it's parenting, housing construction, accounting, you name it, a person must care to be successful and effective. Teaching Annie to care by modeling it for her is a life lesson, as well as a lesson in writing. While I am sure she does care about other things in her life (cookies, friendships, outdoor play), writing isn't on the list. I want to put it there.

Deborah Tannen, a popular author and a linguistics professor at Georgetown University, once said, "There's no understanding without caring" (1988, p. 111). So I spend a few weeks coaching Annie, during which I talk with her about caring in general. We talk about caring for a baby brother or a pet, caring for toys, and caring about how we treat each other. We make a list of ways we show we care about things and people (see Figure 3-1). Then we begin a conversation about applying these principles of caring to the writing work we have to do.

Annie is pleased with her list, as I am. We reread her list, and I ask her to try to make some connections among all the things she does when she cares about things. Annie's answer surprises me; she says she "thinks about it and spends time doing it or thinking about it." Hmm. Yes, that is what we do when we care. And that is

When Annie cares about something, she "thinks about it and spends time doing it or thinking about it." And that is what writers do when they care about writing.

What I care about	How I show it
My baby brother	I hug him when he's scared or tired. I play with him. I make him laugh. I tell him I love him. I protect him. I spend time with him.
My new doll I got for my birthday	I keep her inside so she won't get dirty. I play with her every day. I invite my cousin to play with us. I don't let my brother get her.
Singing	I sing all the time. I watch music videos. I listen to my cousin's iPod. I learn new songs. I make up songs.
My mother	I kiss her in the morning and at night. I try to be good. I help her watch my brother. I dry the dishes for her.
Going to the beach	I count the days until summer. I look at my pail and shovel in the closet. I look at pictures of last summer at the beach.

▲ Figure 3-1 *Annie's ways of showing she cares*

what writers do when they care about writing.

The next point is to ask Annie to imagine what she would do if she cared about writing. Of course, she wrinkles her nose and says she doesn't really care. But she agrees that she will try to figure out what she might do. Looking back at her first list, she thinks about the people and activities she cares about, and we construct a caring chart together (see Figure 3-2).

Ultimately, Annie has proven herself to be quite a thinker. She's invented a good list of ways to get herself to care about writing. We learn from Annie that all students know how to care about something; our work is to transfer that caring to writing. It is unlikely that Annie will go from writing two lines to filling up two pages in a few weeks' time. Nevertheless, she has strategies that can help her to build trust in herself as a writer and ways to put stock in what she has to say. Starting by investing in one of the strategies she's listed, she can begin to develop her caring attitude toward writing.

How does this relate to students in your class? Clearly, we must invest time in teaching them to care. Spending time in conferences and small groups (see Part II) can help them to see that they do care about many things. Then we can help them transfer some of that caring to their writing. They won't love writing overnight, but it will eventually begin to matter to them.

Strategies for Elaboration

We've all done it. We've all sent students back to their seats with directions to "add details" or "write more." Some students dutifully do this. A few add in an adjective or two; others add a line of dialogue. Many just add on a few sentences at the end. Let's face it: Elaborating on writing is something we don't teach often or well enough.

Fortunately, there are many professional books today to help us with this (see sidebar on page 55 for suggestions). If you have not read at least one or two of them, put them on your to-do list immediately. Most of these books center on teaching *craft*. Craft means all the nuances of language, conventions, and structure techniques that writers use to

- Tell a story from my life that excites me

- Think of someone I want to share it with

- Imagine reading it to my mother or brother

- Promise myself a reward at the end of writing (cookies!)

- Imagine making up a song from it (or a game, a TV show, and so on)

- Think about a time I was proud of myself and imagine feeling that way about my writing

- Choose one writing skill and get extra good at it (Annie chooses "finding exciting words")

- Write at home because the teacher isn't there and the writing is all mine

- Keep my writing in a shoebox to give to my brother when he learns to read

- Get better at writing so I won't rush through it

- Find a partner I can trust and share my stories with him or her

- Think of my stories as gifts to my mother; write poems for her

- Find a favorite book and try to write stories like it

- Make a special writing spot in my house and go there every day to write quietly

- Write with a fancy pen, on colored paper or in a special notebook

- Use a timer to write for five minutes, then seven minutes, and build up to more time

Figure 3-2 *Annie's chart of ways to nurture a caring attitude toward writing*

make their writing flow. Elaboration is a subset of craft, because it focuses on the ways writers add information to their writing. I suggest that the best way to teach students—struggling or not—to elaborate on their writing is to study actual texts to see how writers do it.

Elaboration is a subset of craft, because it focuses on the ways writers add information to their writing. I suggest that the best way to teach students—struggling or not—to elaborate on their writing is to study actual texts to see how writers do it.

Day ONE:

> *I like videogames*

Day ONE: Add in WHY.

> *I like videogames because they are fun.*

Day TWO: Add in another character.

> *I like to play videogames with my brother. They are fun.*

Day TWO: Add in a name and add an ending.

> *I like to play videogames with my brother Joel. They are fun.*
> *I always win and Joel gets mad.*

Day THREE: Make a plan for something else you could add to this writing someday in the future.

> 1. *I could add the name of the game.*
>
> 2. *I could add how I play the game.*
>
> 3. *I could add what Joel says when he is mad.*

▲ Figure 3-3 *Annie's writing, going from little writing on the page to adding more*

The Struggling Writer

Selected professional books on teaching craft in writing:

Angelillo, Janet. (2002). *A Fresh Approach to Teaching Punctuation: Helping Young Writers Use Conventions With Precision and Purpose*. New York: Scholastic.

Angelillo, Janet. (2005). *Making Revision Matter: Strategies for Guiding Students to Focus, Organize, and Strengthen Their Writing Independently*. New York: Scholastic.

Culham, Ruth. (2003). *6 + 1 Traits of Writing: The Complete Guide, Grades 3 and Up*. New York: Scholastic.

Dorfman, Lynne R., & Cappelli, Rose. (2007). *Mentor Texts: Teaching Writing Through Children's Literature, K–6*. Portland, ME: Stenhouse.

Fletcher, Ralph, & Portalupi, JoAnn. (2007). *Craft Lessons: Teaching Writing K–8* (2nd ed.). Portland, ME: Stenhouse.

Portalupi, JoAnn, & Fletcher, Ralph. (2001). *Nonfiction Craft Lessons: Teaching Information Writing K–8*. Portland, ME: Stenhouse.

Ray, Katie Wood. (1999). *Wondrous Words: Writers and Writing in the Elementary Classroom*. Urbana, IL: National Council of Teachers of English.

Mentor Texts and What to Do With Them: Reading Like a Writer

For several years, writing teachers have known that teaching students to write using mentor texts is as appropriate for elementary students as it is for MFA students. A mentor text (sometimes called a touchstone text) is any text that a teacher or student studies deeply to learn how it is written. These may include read-aloud picture books, short texts from newspapers or magazines, or parts of longer chapter books. After students know the content of the text, the teacher returns to it with them to study how it is written. Ultimately, we hope students learn to do this on their own with texts of their choosing, but we begin with texts that the teacher selects.

My colleague and mentor Carl Anderson taught me years ago that one ingredient in successful conferring is to have two or three mentor texts that you bring with you to every conference. That way, you always have a model to use when teaching students what writers actually do. In his book *How's It Going? A Practical Guide to Conferring With Writers* (2000), he gives examples of the power of mentor texts and their usefulness in conferences. Since I believe that the strongest teaching for strugglers is in conferring, I hope you will collect a small number of excellent texts to use frequently during conferences. Using the same text repeatedly shows students that even something very familiar can yield new learning when studied through a different lens.

Let's examine a few mentor texts that lend themselves to elaboration. Of course, these same techniques are used in most books, so feel free to use any book of your choice when teaching this. In Figure 3-4, I have listed quotes from the text on the left of the chart and elaboration techniques on the right. With a little work, you could use the right column of my chart and replace the book samples with books of your choice. And certainly you can find texts and elaboration techniques on your own. One caution: Teach only one elaboration technique at a time! Remember that less is more!

The texts I quoted are but a fraction of the texts you can use and a minor fraction of the elaboration techniques that writers use. The important point is to choose a text and study it deeply, over and over again. You will find writing tricks in there that you had not noticed on the first, or even the fifth, reading. Then teach these tricks to your writers.

I also recommend that you get to know at least one children's picture book very well—"by heart," as Katie Ray tells us in her book *What You Know by Heart: How to Develop Curriculum for Your Writing Workshop* (Heinemann, 2002). Katie teaches us that to understand a text we must know it from the inside; cursory and superficial reading will not suffice. When we know a text so well that we can recite it, we begin to find the nuances and get inside the craft of what makes it work. This does not mean that you should sit and memorize books! But when you read something so frequently that it is very familiar to you, you begin to see how the writer made it work and can use it to teach the craft of writing.

The Struggling Writer

▼ Figure 3-4 *Mentor texts and elaboration techniques*

Mentor text: *Prairie Train* by Marsha Wilson Chall	Elaboration techniques
Shhh, listen— Here she comes—*woooOOOO* In the dark I stretch full-out, My ear down to the floor, *Clickety clack clack clack*. The Great Northern rumbles Over frozen tracks. Her headlight sweeps across the field; Broken cornstalks wave hellooOOOO . . . Night chases behind her And hitches a rail. So LOOOoong . . .	• Addressing the audience at beginning ("Shhh, listen—") • Actual sound (of train whistle) mimicked; technique = what do you hear? • Character states what she is doing, followed by detail of how it looks • Statement of what is happening, followed by three examples that show details of event • Personification of surroundings through use of verbs (*sweeps*, *wave*, *chases*) • Two sound responses (follow train whistle) • Use of ellipses that indicate continuing sound

Mentor text: *Rosa* by Nikki Giovanni	Elaboration techniques
And the people walked. They walked in the rain. They walked in the hot sun. They walked early in the morning. They walked late at night. They walked at Christmas, and they walked at Easter. They walked on the Fourth of July; they walked on Labor Day. They walked on Thanksgiving, and then it was almost Christmas again. They still walked.	• Deliberate repetition of the same sentence beginning ("They walked . . .") • Juxtaposing opposites (rain . . . hot sun) • Adding in the weather • Adding in the time of day • Marking the passage of time through use of seasons and/or holidays • Developing a seesaw rhythm to sentences and using it to write more (First we did this, and then we did that . . .)

(continued on page 58)

Mentor text: *Salt in His Shoes: Michael Jordan in Pursuit of a Dream* by Deloris Jordan with Roslyn M. Jordan	Elaboration techniques
"Everything," Mama replied, and she hugged him. "Now go wash up and tell your brothers and sisters to get ready for dinner." Michael dashed out of the kitchen, almost knocking over his father, who was walking in. "What's he up to now?" asked Daddy. "Oh, the usual," laughed Mama, "chasing a dream."	• Adding an action to a line of dialogue • Connecting the title to something that happens in the story • Dialogue that shows people in real situations (notice how Mama talks)

Obviously, all writers benefit from this type of writing instruction, and I urge you to make it an important part of your writing curriculum, but the benefits for strugglers can be enormous. At the very least, you can prod them by taking out the mentor text again and suggesting that they look at the ways the writer has elaborated. It's a good way to find more to write.

Stretching Students' Stamina for Writing

I need to be clear that this book is not meant for teaching students who suffer from specific learning difficulties. When I write here about stretching stamina, it is not to say that I have the solution for attention deficit disorder or difficulties of that nature. There are other research and professional texts filled with information on those issues. I am writing about the student in the regular education classroom who quickly gets tired or bored, or who cannot write for a long time. That is the type of stamina we'll deal with in this section.

I began to think seriously about stamina years ago when I realized that for some students, the only time they sat for a sustained period of time to write was during the state writing tests! Of course, the tests were torturous for them because they had no staying power. I noticed that many students can't sustain writing for short blocks of time, let alone a full 45 minutes. Many writing teachers have addressed this issue since then, including Lucy Calkins and Ralph Fletcher. However, despite the work done to improve stamina, some young writers remain unable to stay the course for even a short block of time.

As with any other skill—playing an instrument, practicing a sport, exercising, painting, gardening—building stamina takes time and patience. In fact, sometimes it makes your bones or muscles hurt. Stamina is hard to build!

Earlier in this chapter, I listed ways to use mentor texts to encourage young writers to elaborate on their writing. Having many ways to get a job done is one way to build stamina for it. But other ways exist as well, such as making a plan, thinking about time management, and stretching oneself every day. Students need time to grasp what stamina is and why it's important; then they need coaching in it.

Like Annie, from the first part of this chapter, Moises is a student who writes as little as possible. He's a third grader who would rather roam than write. When I visit his class to observe him, at his teacher's request, I notice he ambles around the room before sitting at his desk to write, sits on his legs and almost falls off his chair, and sharpens three pencils before even thinking about writing. Moises may need assistance in several areas, but he definitely needs to work on stamina.

His teacher and I sit with him for a conference. He shrugs his shoulders and yawns often enough that we worry about whether he's getting enough sleep. Of course, he may be telling us he's bored, but we'll rule out other problems first. Writing requires both physical and mental stamina, so his teacher assures me she'll talk to his mother about his eating and sleeping routines. Nevertheless, we decide to work on building his stamina for the task of writing, knowing that this type of stamina is needed in all academic areas.

First I ask Moises what he likes to do during writing time.

"Draw," he replies.

"Good," I say. "Today I'm going to ask you to draw for three minutes. I don't want you to stop until I tell you to, but I want you to think about how it feels to keep yourself going with your drawing."

Moises starts to draw a picture of himself at the park while I keep an eye on the clock. He looks up at me a few times, and I nod for him to just keep going. I want him to recognize that as he draws he is directing himself to keep going, even though he usually doesn't think about it at all. At the end of three minutes, I stop him.

"Okay, tell me what you were thinking as you drew your picture."

Moises knits his brow and then says, "I was thinking about the picture and about going to the park yesterday."

"What else?"

"Well . . . I was thinking that I went on the slide so I have to put that in the picture."

"Terrific!" I say. "Moises, you have just figured out one way to build stamina in your writing. When you have to keep going, you think of what else to put in."

Moises does not look convinced. He tells me he has no trouble drawing but that writing is not fun for him. I tell him that writing may not be fun, but if he builds up his stamina it won't be so exhausting for him.

Over the next eight weeks, I see Moises for a conference once a week. His mother has indicated that he has no problem with sleeping or eating at home, so we assume that his yawning is connected to his trouble with writing. I work with him on building stamina, knowing that there are many skills he needs in addition to this one, but that without stamina, Moises cannot improve his writing. Using his skill as a sketcher, we make a list for how to keep going (see Figure 3-5).

In another class, I share Moises's list with Precious. She is easily distracted and has trouble getting much down on the page. She agrees that Moises's suggestions are good, but there are too many for her. Once again, I am reminded that we must teach less, not more! So I ask Precious to choose one stamina strategy from Moises's list for us to work on. Then

The Struggling Writer

1. Start out with three minutes and add a minute to your work time every day.

2. At the end of the work time, think back on how it felt to work that long.

3. Use something you can do well to teach you how to keep going.

4. Think about a time you "got lost" in doing something you like; imagine yourself getting lost in writing.

5. Practice writing at home for five minutes every day.

6. When you finish your writing, jot down what you will start with the next day so you can get going quickly.

7. Don't get discouraged if you have a bad day; you'll be better the next day.

8. Name three ways you get yourself to keep going (set a goal of number of lines, keep writing until you hear a chime, don't keep looking at the clock).

9. Bring a bottle of water to school so you can take a drink without leaving your seat.

10. Think of physical activity after writing as a break and reward for hard writing work.

Figure 3-5 *Student's list of ways to build stamina*

Precious decides that none of those strategies will work for her, and I realize I am picking up true resistance.

This is one of the few times that I've met overt resistance. I confess that when I work with reluctant students, they usually enjoy the one-on-one attention they get from me and the lack of sparring between us. Over many years, I have learned never to argue with students, because they usually win! I'm the one who gets angry and goes home with a headache! No, going head to head doesn't work, so this child is challenging me to figure out new ways to overcome her reluctance. Do I have the stamina to do it?

It is easy to slip into a usual pattern of "try this and try that," but I can see that this student has set her jaw and won't budge. Sometimes it is best to walk away and try again the next day; we never know when a student has had some trouble at home or perhaps has a mild upset stomach or whatever. But when resistance is a pattern, it is time to do serious work on it.

So this time, I say to Precious, "You know, I'm really stumped. I had hoped I could help you build some stamina for your work, but I don't know what to say. Can you help me figure this out?"

Precious looks at me incredulously. "Why don't you tell me to just do it?" she asks.

"Would that work?" I ask her, smiling.

She raises her eyebrows and says, "No. But I could write more if I had a contest."

"Explain what you mean."

"You know, I could write if I was trying to write more than someone else, or if I was racing the clock or something like that."

Precious is a competitor! With no competition, she's not inclined to perform. So we find another student who is willing to compete with her once a week. Precious tells me she'll look forward to taking part in a contest in writing fast or writing longer or writing the most dialogue or using the longest word. At other times, she'll do her best to practice writing to get ready for the weekly contest.

What we learn from Precious is not that we should turn our writing instruction into a competition, but that students can often come up with their own remedies for difficult situations. We must invite them into the work of figuring out solutions. Too often, we take all the work on our shoulders, while students know exactly what they need to do. Asking them to get onboard with figuring out answers to problems is a good way to teach them to think and to problem-solve for themselves. If I have trouble exercising, ultimately only I can figure out what will get me to do it, because the solution has to work for me. Understanding themselves as learners shows students that learning is a journey of self-discovery.

We must invite them into the work of figuring out solutions. Too often, we take all the work on our shoulders, while students know exactly what they need to do.

The Struggling Writer

Let's face it: Practice is not always fun. It is only when we've gained some proficiency at a skill that the practice begins to be enjoyable. Think of those first few years practicing the piano and you remember how dry and boring practice can be. How the minutes dragged!

But without practice, it is hard to build stamina in anything. Therefore, take time from the beginning of the year to build stamina for all children in both reading and writing. Start with a short period of writing, or two short periods per day. Build that up to more. Talk about how it feels to stretch yourself to do more, including what makes it hard to do so. Encourage each other; ask partners to cheerlead for each other. Let the community know that all learners need the support of the class to grow in strength, knowledge, and writing wisdom.

Summary

We've seen that most students who feel they have nothing to say usually have lots going on but don't know how to translate that into writing. Using techniques such as talking, sketching, and staying with one story for a long time, we can build confidence in these writers. Once students know that their ideas are worthwhile and are expandable, they are ready to learn strategies for making their ideas into longer writing.

To-do list for teachers:

- Think about yourself as a writer and figure out what obstacles you put in the way of your own writing.

- Using your list of obstacles, figure out how you could overcome each one.

- Study the craft in one or two well-written children's books.

- Read a professional book on teaching craft: You might start with Katie Ray's *Wondrous Words* and then go to Ralph Fletcher and JoAnn Portalupi's *Craft Lessons*.

- Practice craft in your own writing so you have actual experience in what you are teaching.

"Does punctuation count?"

Teaching Students Who Struggle With Written Conventions

I frequently tell the story of an eighth-grade student many years ago who gave me a 10-page paper with no punctuation. After I handed it back to her with shock and dismay, she said, "Oh, Mrs. A, you're so good at it. Just put it in wherever you want!"

That event sent me on my quest to understand why my teaching of conventions wasn't successful, which continued after I wrote *A Fresh Approach to Teaching Punctuation: Helping Young Writers Use Conventions With Precision and Purpose* (2002). Now, I see little reason for students to ignore conventions, and I have worked with many teachers to teach students to enjoy punctuating their writing. However, the truth is that many struggling writers remain confused about punctuation, grammar, and spelling. The written conventions of language make for added stress and become details these students have trouble remembering. I can understand why they depend on their teachers to fill it in: We seem to care about it, and we're good at it! So they let us do that work for them, since it matters to us more than it does to them.

Of course, we know that conventions are more than a series of rules we impose on writers. Writers can no more write without punctuation than painters can paint without canvas. (Yes, I know there are exceptions, but we'll not focus on them here.) Writers use conventions to make meaning, to shape sentences and inflection, to create surprise and rhythm. When students do not understand this, or when they've been taught that conventions are a bunch of rules to obey, their writing, and their ability to make meaning, suffer. In fact, it usually remains stilted, voiceless, and as boring to read as it is to write. How we all suffer!

In Chapter 1, we looked briefly at supporting students with spelling instruction. In this chapter, we'll look at a few ways to support strugglers as they wrestle to understand punctuation and grammar:

- Punctuation inquiry and ongoing study
- Individual work in punctuation and grammar
- Studying mentor sentences for models of rhythm

Punctuation Inquiry and Ongoing Study

Teachers often show me student writing that has one similar trait: It begins with a capital letter at the top of the page and goes on in one long sentence until it ends with a period. There is no punctuation between the beginning and the end, and the teachers are exasperated. I've taken to looking at this writing positively—at least these students know that a capital letter comes at the beginning of a piece of writing and a period means "the end"—but teachers who see this repeatedly are not amused by it. They teach it again and again; they remind students again and again; they may even correct it again and again. And still the errors remain.

I've observed that young writers who do not use punctuation or grammar to help them shape meaning as they read also do not use punctuation and grammar when writing. This is a broad generalization with many exceptions, but it is often true. Students need to have their awareness of punctuation and grammar heightened. We expect students to know these things, we think we teach them, but we often do not talk about them in deep and thoughtful ways. The old story about Oscar Wilde spending the morning putting a comma in and the afternoon taking it out is still relevant when we consider how carefully writers use punctuation. The following vignette illustrates how we can begin to break through the conventions barrier.

In a third-grade classroom, I work with three students who have been identified by their teacher as "conventions strugglers." I am amused that something as small as punctuation is so great a stumbling block for these students and for their teacher. They don't bother with it; he considers their writing unreadable without it. Tempers rage, and the scene becomes ugly at times. For me, punctuation is like ice cream—I can't live without it. So teaching it to these students will be interesting and engaging.

I gather the three students—Jack, Mikey, and Andrea—and ask their teacher to sit with us at a round table. I want him to notice how these students can learn to approximate using punctuation after one or two sessions of inquiry. I choose a book that the teacher has recently read aloud to the students, and I photocopy one page of the text for them to study with me. First I read the page aloud to them to refresh their memories, and we spend a minute recalling the plot. Then I tell them to reread the page and to notice the punctuation on the page, even if they don't know what it is called. They seem relieved not to be quizzed on the names of the punctuation marks and to simply point to what they find. Then I reread each sentence and ask them to listen to my voice. I ask them to listen to what the punctuation mark tells my voice to do as I read the words. We begin a chart listing what they hear (see Figure 4-1).

In a short time, we've investigated and discovered meanings for two types of punctuation. Clearly, this is not everything they need to know, but again, less is more.

Punctuation mark	What we heard and what it means	Example from a book	Example from our writing	"The rule"
. = period	It makes your voice go down at the end of a sentence. It means the sentence is finished.			Put a period at the end of every sentence.
"------" = quotation marks	Read the words with the character's voice. They show you that the words came out of the talker's mouth.			Put quotation marks at the beginning and end of the words that a character says.

▲ Figure 4-1 *Helping struggling writers learn to "hear" punctuation*

I prefer they learn to use a little punctuation correctly than be handed the meaning and functions of 20 types of punctuation that go right over their heads.

When I leave the group to confer with other students, I tell them that I want them to write a few sentences on any topic. When I return, I want to hear about the punctuation choices they have made and the reasons why. My emphasis on the purpose of punctuation is to convince them that punctuation is used to create meaning when writing, not sprinkled on at the end. We *compose* in sentences; we don't just write words and add the punctuation later.

> *We compose in sentences; we don't just write words and add the punctuation later.*

The strength of this process lies in the opportunity to slow students down and let them reflect. Too often, punctuation and grammar instruction is too abstract for young ones. Allowing them to stay with one page of text and reflect on it in terms of punctuation gives them a chance to see it with new eyes. This process will not make them punctuation and grammar experts overnight, but it will help them discover—rather than be told—the power of punctuation as they read and write.

One important ingredient of success in conventions is to talk about them frequently. Teachers often feel they have taught conventions or that students should have learned

Professional books that support teaching punctuation and grammar:

Anderson, Jeff. (2005). *Mechanically Inclined: Building Grammar, Usage, and Style into Writer's Workshop*. Portland, ME: Stenhouse.

Anderson, Jeff. (2007). *Everyday Editing: Inviting Students to Develop Skill and Craft in Writer's Workshop*. Portland, ME: Stenhouse.

Angelillo, Janet. (2002). *A Fresh Approach to Teaching Punctuation: Helping Young Writers Use Conventions With Precision and Purpose*. Portland, ME: Stenhouse.

Angelillo, Janet. (2008). *Grammar Study: Helping Students Get What Grammar Is and How It Works*. New York: Scholastic.

Ehrenworth, Mary, & Vinton, Vicki. (2005). *The Power of Grammar: Unconventional Approaches to the Conventions of Language*. Portsmouth, NH: Heinemann.

Feigelson, Dan. (2008). *Practical Punctuation: Lessons on Rule Making and Rule Breaking in Elementary Writing*. Portsmouth, NH: Heinemann.

Smith, Michael W., & Wilhelm, Jeffrey D. (2007). *Getting It Right: Fresh Approaches to Teaching Grammar, Usage, and Correctness*. New York: Scholastic.

Topping, Donna H., & Hoffman, Sandra J. (2006). *Getting Grammar: 150 New Ways to Teach an Old Subject*. Portsmouth, NH: Heinemann.

Weaver, Constance. (1996). *Teaching Grammar in Context*. Portsmouth, NH: Heinemann.

them in previous years, and then expect a degree of proficiency above the students' level. In the real world, writers talk about punctuation all the time; for example, I will call my writer friend Shirley and ask her if she prefers a particular sentence with a comma or a semicolon in it. We'll talk about my purpose, how I want it to sound, and my menu of possible choices. We don't take time for students to have these conversations because we treat punctuation and grammar as a matter of right or wrong. Having a conversation with the class or a small group where you "wrestle" together to figure out the punctuation is a wonderful model for students who fear or avoid the work that goes into negotiating meaning.

Like any sophisticated skill, learning punctuation is a process. Here are suggestions for supporting strugglers as they work on conventions.

- Using grade-appropriate literature, lead students through an inquiry into what messages writers give readers when they use punctuation.

- Focus on how particular punctuation marks help readers access meaning (i.e., that each mark is a symbol for something). At this point, do not focus on the rules.

- Allow students to use their own words to create a chart of punctuation meanings with exact examples from literature to support their thinking.

- Give students time to practice punctuation in their notebooks, both in entries they've already written and as they compose new entries.

- Ask students to talk (or write) about specific punctuation decisions they've made in their writing. Ask what they were trying to communicate to their readers by using that punctuation. They might refer back to ways a particular author used the same punctuation marks.

- Add student writing samples to the chart and offer opportunity for conversation about them.

- Ask students to look in other texts to find more uses for each mark as well as other examples of the same uses.

- Discuss how some authors seem to use punctuation more formally than others. Use examples from literature to illustrate this. Discuss what this might mean for their work.

- Explore the idea of using a mentor author to learn punctuation and discuss ways to choose that author wisely.

- Discuss the possible punctuation differences among genres (e.g., e-mail is less formal than a science report). Look at literature examples across genres to illustrate this. Talk about what that means for students' own work in school.

- Give students opportunities to practice taking dictation with a partner.

- Dictate a few sentences to the class and collect their work to quickly assess which students need extra support.

- Consider organizing small guided writing groups for students who are having trouble or for those who are ready for more sophisticated work.

- Ask students to talk in reading conferences about ways they've used punctuation to figure out the meaning of a text.

- Ask students to talk in writing conferences about punctuation decisions they've made.

- Choose selected sentences from texts as ways to teach students to write longer sentences.

- Discuss the idea of automaticity. Sometimes writers think about each comma, but usually they compose quickly, without thinking about the period at the end of each sentence, just as musicians don't think about each rest in a piece of music.

- Finally, bring out the style manuals or textbooks and ask students to find each punctuation rule. Add the formal rules to the chart beside the student language. Give them time to process this and to talk about the formal language of the rules.

- Create a rubric with students that will offer opportunities for them to explain some of the punctuation choices they've made.

The Struggling Writer

Individual Work in Punctuation and Grammar

In Chapter 11, we will study the importance of conferring for all writers, especially strugglers. Some of the conferences you plan should be "conventions conferences." Below is the transcript of a conference I had with Jack, one of the third-grade students from the small study group in this chapter.

Teacher: Jack, talk to me about how you are using punctuation in your writing today.

Jack: Well . . . I'm putting some periods in, I guess.

Teacher: Good, good. That means you remember what we did last time when we thought about the way periods make sentences sound.

Jack: Uh-huh.

Teacher: Okay, so you are being careful to put in all the periods you need. What else are you thinking about in terms of punctuation?

Jack: [silent for a good minute while I wait and smile] Hmm . . . maybe questions?

Teacher: Super! You know that sometimes writers use question marks when they have to write a question. I'm glad you've been paying attention to other punctuation as you read. Good work!

Jack: Uh-huh.

Teacher: I have an article here from *Muse* magazine, and I know it has a few questions in it. Let's look at them, okay?

Jack: Sure.

Teacher: [I take out the magazine and open to an article that I know begins with three questions.] So, last week, you listened when I read to you, and we figured out how periods sound. Today, listen to this and tell me how question marks sound. [I read the three questions.]

Jack: Your voice sounded different.

Teacher: Tell me what you mean by that.

Jack: Your voice went higher.

Teacher: Yes, that's exactly how it sounds when we ask questions. Our voices go higher. So now when you are reading or writing, if you want your voice to go higher to ask a question, put a question mark to show that to us.

Jack: Okay.

Teacher: So, Jack, your work for today is to try to write one or two questions in your writing so you can practice using question marks. Even if you end up taking the questions out later, it still is good practice to try that now. So tell me what you are going to do.

Jack: [repeats my instructions and keeps a copy of the article so he can refer to it]

Notice that Jack is still struggling. He gives me answers he hopes will appease me. Also notice that I remain positive and upbeat at all times. The possibility of Jack's not getting what I am teaching him is not even a blip on the screen. My attitude is "Of course you can do this! You are a thinker, just as I am." Notice also the wait time I give him. I don't jump in with the answers, because that will only teach him to be more dependent on the teacher. In addition, whatever he says shapes where I go with the conference. Even though I may prefer to teach him something more jazzy or original, if Jack wants to learn question marks, then that's what I will teach him. Jack can't wiggle out of the work, but I do give him tiny steps to help him. I don't upbraid him for his continued shakiness on periods. I know he will get there. It will click. But he must feel that he can do this. It's crucial to take small steps with great kindness and support.

> *My attitude is "Of course you can do this! You are a thinker, just as I am."*

The Struggling Writer

Mikey shows me his work at the end of the class. He has started to add in periods as large as acorns. This is fine, and at some point he will make them appropriately smaller. For now, he is quite proud of the periods, even though not every one is in the correct place. Andrea has asked her teacher if she can use a marker for the periods in her writing, so all of them are pink. Again, this is fine for now. Eventually, the need for pink punctuation will wane, while we hope the use of punctuation will not.

At this point, I recommend individual cheat sheets for some strugglers. For example, many of us keep to-do lists; mine tend to be long and detailed, and I enjoy crossing off each item once it's accomplished. The school version of this is "editing sheets." But I have seen too many students just skim the sheets and check off items without even rereading their writing! We need a better system for editing than this. Students who struggle with conventions may easily be discouraged by long lists of rules to follow and check. We can make this more doable by limiting the number of items on the lists and by asking students to choose a small number of points to add to their lists. These points on the list should be specific to the needs of struggling students and composed in a conference or small group with the teacher and a group of students (see Figure 4-2). These lists should be revised as students become comfortable with items they formerly struggled to learn. The minor inconvenience to the teacher of some students using a different editing checklist from the majority of the class is well worth the benefits.

Sometimes teachers ask me what I think of worksheets in grammar and punctuation, and I tell them I find it hard to imagine how preprinted worksheets can meet the individual needs of students. These sheets often contain regional differences in language and spelling. I remember phonics sheets I once used that insisted *hog* rhymes with *dog*. Nope, I'm a New Yawkah—it's "dawg." Anyway, worksheets have limited usefulness in classrooms that focus on authentic learning and literature, but I am always open to possibilities. Certainly, used carefully and sparingly, these resources can be helpful for some. But no student should be sent off to do reams of worksheets because

> *It is hard to imagine how preprinted worksheets can meet the individual needs of students.*

Name: MIKEY	I didn't do this at all	I did this sometimes	I mostly did this	I got it!
Punctuation at end of sentences				
Quotation marks for talking				
Capital letters for names				
Capital letters for sentence beginnings				

▲ Figure 4-2 *Student's individual editing sheet*

he is struggling, or even if he's not. In my mind, this amounts to teaching malpractice, but the thoughtful use of an occasional worksheet, or even a section of one to emphasize or reiterate a learned point, is acceptable. Just be wise and wary.

Today's teachers are stretched very thin. There is so much to do and so little time. One possibility for finding assistance is to ask for community volunteers (especially retired teachers) or to enlist older students who need or want to do community service. When you have the benefit of aid, be specific about how these people can help. For example, volunteers must not correct students' writing or in any way make them feel inadequate. But talking out their writing plans with a volunteer or aide before writing can help strugglers' build confidence and writing capacity. For example, a student says to an aide before writing, "This is my sentence, and I think I need an apostrophe and a question mark." The aide or volunteer can encourage the student by helping her think through her writing before actually doing it.

Studying Mentor Sentences for Models of Rhythm

In my book *Grammar Study* (Angelillo, 2008a), I wrote about teaching students to hear the "music" of sentences. Punctuation and grammar are similar to harmony and counterpoint in music. We can enjoy a good story, as we enjoy a good song, but we enjoy it all the more once we know how it works. Musicians study the way music works, and writers and readers study the way language works.

Struggling writers usually don't operate at this degree of sophistication. But let's assume they are intellectually curious—perhaps because we have encouraged them to be so—about language and how it works. That would lead us to invite them into what Frank

How to use volunteers effectively:

• Spend time teaching them the particular angle you want them to take with strugglers: kindness, positive attitude, teaching independence, letting students make decisions to build confidence.

• Have them work with a limited number of students on a limited number of strategies.

• Ask them to become familiar with what you have taught in your whole-class instruction.

• Ask them to focus on ONE strategy with learners; often, they see so many things to "correct" that they overload students.

• Ask them to keep a record of what they have taught and assigned to students so you can follow up.

• Assess their relationship with their students—whether students are thriving under their guidance—and reassign them as necessary.

• Coach them as necessary; often they come with big hearts, but they need our encouragement to do their best for students and to feel successful themselves.

Smith (1987) has long called "the literacy club." If we did this, we might change the way we perform in class, as well as student performance. For example, we might express our own ongoing delight at interesting words, onomatopoeia, the way puns and jokes play with language, and, of course, beautiful sentences. In his *New York Times* editorial after the death of writer John Updike, Verlyn Klinkenborg said, "You can read him for his books, but it's better to read him for his sentences, any one of which—anywhere—can rise up to startle you with its wry perfection" (p. A26). Are we ever startled by the perfection of sentences? Do we read fiction and nonfiction looking for the gorgeous or melodic sentence to share with students? Or do we sink into a morass of complaint about how badly students write, when we've not shown them how beautifully they *could* write? For those who whine about the state of language today, it is our duty to model for students our own exuberant joy in language. I remain amazed at my own grown children, who today still love "the King's English" and Shakespeare because they grew up hearing me read to them from the King James Bible every night before bed. They love language that falls trippingly from their tongues.

Of course, I am not suggesting you feed your third graders a diet of John Updike. There are many writers of children's literature whose sentences could also "startle you with [their] wry perfection." I have been startled by the prose and poetry of Pam Munoz Ryan, Naomi Shihab Nye, E. B. White, Karen Hesse, Richard Peck, Gary Paulsen, Eloise Greenfield, Christopher Paul Curtis, and a host of others. Read children's books looking for beautiful sentences—not just the long, complex ones, but also the short, elegant ones. Too often we read looking for the comprehension questions we'll ask students, or the literary elements we'll quiz them on. Let's also read looking for great sentences to be our models for the art of writing.

Here is what to do with a sample sentence:

- Explain to a small group of strugglers that you are going to study how sentences sound when they are read aloud.

- Choose a simple sentence from a familiar book and repeat it several times, using the same inflection and emphasizing the punctuation.

- Display the sentence on chart paper or a whiteboard and ask the students to read the sentence as you repeat it.

- Sweep your hand under the sentence as you read it, but pause to point to the punctuation.

- Ask students to talk about how the sentence sounds.

- Model how you can change one word at a time in the sentence and still keep the same rhythm and punctuation, because sentences have construction, not just random words.

    1. "Where's Papa going with that ax?" (from E. B. White, *Charlotte's Web*, p. 1)

    2. Where's Papa going with that dog?

    3. Where's Joey going with that dog?

    4. When's Joey going with that dog?

    5. When's Joey playing with that dog?

    6. Why's Joey playing with that dog?

    7. Why's Mary playing with that dog?

    8. Why's Mary playing with the dog?

    9. Why's Mary singing to the cat?

- Help students to do the same thing, emphasizing that the structure and punctuation of the sentence remain the same while the words change.

- Ask students to practice this on their own or with partners, first orally and then writing down some of their practice sentences (including the punctuation).

- Continue to look for sentences that have structures you would like students to learn; remember that "hearing" the sentence and the punctuation will give strugglers support in writing complete sentences, though, frankly, this works for all students.

Enemy Pie by Derek Munson	*Come On, Rain!* by Karen Hesse	*The House in the Night* by Susan Marie Swanson
"It should have been a perfect summer." (p. 1) It should have been a lovely summer. It should have been a snowy winter. That should have been a snowy weekend.	"I hug Mamma hard, and she hugs me back." * I squeeze Teddy hard, and he squeezes me back. I hold Mamma's hand, and she holds me back. Mamma holds me, and I hold her back.	"Here is the key to the house." * Here is the door of the house. Here is the kitchen of the house. Here is the bed of the bedroom. Here is the remote of the TV.

* unpaginated

▲ Figure 4-3 *Sample sentences from picture books, with ways to change the words to new sentences*

Summary

Students are sometimes identified as struggling writers if they have difficulty with written conventions or grammar. We must remember that some grammatical errors are the result of regional or ethnic language differences, and we must respect that while gently correcting it. We also must teach grammar and punctuation with humor and a sense of discovery. If we communicate exasperation to students, they will respond with resentment, resistance, or humiliation. The best way to deal with mechanical errors is by using authentic literature to model and provide purposeful practice.

To-do list for teachers:

- Study students' use of conventions to see what they are approximating as well as doing correctly.

- Study picture books to determine how writers use punctuation and grammar to express meaning.

- Show that punctuation marks are symbols to tell us how to read the written words.

The Struggling Writer

- Write a sentence from the read-aloud book on a chart and ask students to talk with partners about the conventions in the sentence and/or what is correct about the grammar and punctuation.

- Point out when a writer you are studying does something unconventional and explain why the writer did it and whether or not you want students to try this.

- Schedule regular conferences about conventions, focusing on what students are approximating, attempting, or ready to learn.

- Choose one accessible rule, post it, and then give students a week to gather examples from independent reading books; add their samples to the chart.

- Let students put in punctuation with markers, glitter pens, stickers, or whatever delights them.

- Showcase learning-in-progress; bulletin boards may display writing that is imperfect when students write on an attached colored index card what else they would do. For example, "The next time I will work on . . ."; "This time I learned to . . ."; "I'm proud of adding in periods and capitals . . ."; "This is the first time I put in . . ."; "Next time I will work on apostrophes. . . ." These examples of learning in progress show students becoming aware of what else they must learn. When we demand perfection for bulletin board displays, we often make writing just too difficult and risky for some writers.

▲ Figure 4-4 *Other ways to support use of written conventions*

- Be careful not to use language about punctuation that is too abstract for children. (Classic example: "A sentence is a complete thought." What does that mean to an eight-year-old?)

- In your own notebook, think about how you use punctuation and how you might expand your knowledge of it.

- Read one of the many newer books on punctuation and prepare to be surprised at how it is changing in our global world.

5

"I like it the way it is"

~

Struggling With the Writing Process Itself

I first learned to cook in my mother's kitchen under her watchful eye. I was convinced in those years that cooking was other people's work: I could eat at Mom's house, the college cafeteria, or just do takeout. An hour sweating at a stove and then cleaning up the mess wasn't attractive at all. But Mom insisted I learn, and that was that. When she suggested more salt, I added pepper. She suggested more baking time; I said I liked it the way it was. She suggested baking rolls to go with dinner; I served cookies. More than once I served half-cooked meat—yuck. Something wasn't clicking for me, and Mom just rolled her eyes knowingly.

Mom had taught me some basics, but once I was on my own in my first apartment I was convinced I could invent shortcuts to her long process of making a roast or soup or what we called gravy (red sauce). I was headstrong (and still am). The first time I made baked potatoes, I thought it was ridiculous to cut neat *X*'s in them, as Mom did. I just popped them in the oven. Of course, when they exploded an hour later, I realized Mom was right. Then, when I made rice, I imagined that a cup of rice was too little, so I made three cups, and, like in that old episode of *I Love Lucy,* spent frantic minutes trying to scoop it all up from the floor. The mishaps continued until I surrendered and bought a cookbook. It was time to minimize the messes.

We know that some students resist the process of writing as much as I resisted the process of cooking. Their resistance may be the types we've examined in earlier chapters, or combinations of difficulties. We also know many students who resist by shutting down and insisting that they "like it the way it is." These students may be bored with writing, or they may genuinely know no strategies for writing more or revising their writing.

I suggest going back to the concept of self-regulation for these students. Even students who like their writing the way it is can be required to show they've tried one or more planning or revision strategies, whether or not they ultimately use the revision in their final drafts. In this chapter, we'll look at ways to help young writers understand that liking something the way it is doesn't mean that we can't challenge ourselves to make it better. As a cook, I liked my chicken soup the way it was, but—wow—was it better when Mom convinced me to add onions and salt! Let's help students add onions and salt to their writing.

Revisiting the Writing Process

When Donald Murray, Donald Graves, Lucy Calkins, and others began to teach the writing process in the 1980s, it was based on observations of the actual process professional writers use to produce their writing. The writing-process pioneers were clear that not all writers follow this process exactly, but that many writers do. They suggested it as a way to make students experience authentic writing. The process of finding a meaningful topic, making it important by nurturing the thought, planning and drafting, then revising and editing, is worthwhile for young writers. The writing pioneers did not, however, intend for the process to become a lockstep movement that everyone in the class needed to follow all the time or altogether. It was a guideline, but it was flexible enough to allow for individual needs and creativity.

More than 20 years later, writing process is common in many classrooms. This is excellent news. However, with the institutionalizing of any process comes the simplifying or codifying of it. Teachers are increasingly requiring students to follow the steps of the writing process, but the reasons for the steps, and the thinking behind them, is often absent. I fear that making all students move step by step through the process has contributed to the "I like it the way it is" phenomenon. Some students don't understand or recognize the importance of each step. Others know they can capitalize on the teacher's inclination to respect their choices, so they refuse further work by claiming to "like it that way." The benefit of time and units of study that provide deep instruction over several weeks is lost on students who do not have the habit of mind to do the work that good writing requires.

Let's review the writing process, probably for the hundredth time. However, for each step of the process, let's look at the rationale behind it and what students should learn from it as thinkers as well as writers.

There are many thinking skills that the writing process addresses. For the student who is bored or overwhelmed, we can understand why he or she likes it just the way it is. It's another way of saying that they don't want to dig into the hard work of writing. Frankly, the "old way" of producing a "sloppy copy" on Monday, then fixing the punctuation and rewriting it by Friday, was much less labor- and thinking-intensive, and we can see why students (and, sadly, some teachers) might prefer that. But it does not yield thorough, thinking writers.

I believe it is important for us to explicitly inform students of the thinking strategies behind each step of the process. For some, it seems like we're making them go through a bunch of hoops just to write about their day at the beach. If our conferring and whole-class teaching focuses on "how you learn to think," it may mean more to them.

Steps of the writing process	How it translates into thinking and writing
Selecting a topic	Trusting one's thinking; sorting and sifting; matching idea to genre; generating ideas
Nurturing an idea	Thinking deeply about something; creating and attaching importance to it; dismissing it if necessary; thinking globally about it; thinking specifically about it; planning writing by listing, outlining, organizing; planning genre and audience
Drafting	Putting ideas together for the first time in a written form; doing preliminary work with an expectation of expanding on it; knowing that a first effort does not need to be perfect; expecting that writing will produce more thinking about the topic
Revising	Going back to reread writing; studying and using qualities of good writing; figuring out what else you want to say; using craft; studying a mentor text and applying to writing; considering the reader and his or her understanding of the piece; practicing rethinking; possibly changing meaning
Editing	Rereading for sense; using knowledge of conventions to clarify meaning; respecting the reader; preparing a piece for the public; examining each word and sentence carefully and slowly
Publishing	Sharing and enjoying the responses of readers; making plans for additional writing or future writing goals

Alicia is a second grader who appears to like writing. When I meet with her, she's written a story about an accident in the schoolyard (see Figure 5-2, page 86). It is hard to understand what she's written because the events are not in order, and the point of the piece is not evident until the end, when the victim is in the nurse's office. Alicia's teacher and I ask her to read the writing to us, and she can hardly read it. We suggest that she retell the story, and we'll number the events so she can reorder them. Alicia tells us the story but refuses to change the order of events in the writing. She likes it "the way it is." Sigh.

The following week's conference is a rerun of the previous one. Alicia does not want to change her topic or alter the writing in any way. We recognize that she has worked hard to write the pages she has done, but we hope to teach her something about revision. Eventually, Alicia agrees to divide her story in half—the part in the schoolyard and the part in the nurse's office—and to make one sentence on one page clearer. The strategy we suggest for clarification is to make sure she tells us which character is speaking.

But our concern is less with this particular piece of writing than with teaching Alicia that going back and changing writing is not as painful as it seems; ultimately, Alicia had a revision breakthrough.

Beginning with small changes is helpful for students, but eventually they need to move on to broader changes. It is hard to know if Alicia's first draft is so jumbled because she

- Add one word to your writing.

- Put a star in the margin where you might add a sentence.

- Tell your partner about a part of the story you left out.

- Imagine a sound word you could add to the writing.

- Think about how things in the story smell (or sound) and add that in the margin.

- Use numbers to change the order of events without rewriting the story.

- Reread the pronouns and change some of them to names.

Figure 5-1 *Small steps for building confidence in revisiting writing*

doesn't know where to start. Perhaps she doesn't want to mark up her writing, or perhaps the task seems too daunting for her. Writing on a computer or cutting and taping can make this easier. I also recommend that we not require students to recopy their writing all the time. Sometimes just telling us the changes they would make is enough.

What about the other steps of the process? Some students choose the first idea that pops into their minds and insist on writing about that. It may be a fine idea, but often it is something that doesn't lead to rich writing. Teaching students to constantly keep lists of ideas and to choose from them is helpful. Of course, the life story (see Chapter 2) is useful as well, but only if the student is willing to nurture it to gain new insights.

Students who want to write a draft immediately—and write only one draft—do not understand the process. Doing this is analogous to looking up the answer to a math problem without doing the thinking work to get it. The answer matters less than the ways we think about math. Writing works the same way. While I love to celebrate published work, it matters less to me than what students learn about thinking and mining an idea as they write.

Students who want to write a draft immediately—and write only one draft—do not understand the process. Doing this is analogous to looking up the answer to a math problem without doing the thinking work to get it.

Alicia's first draft

Alicia

We played for lunch. The chair had blood. It was in the schoolyard. Maya was crying. Then the teacher was there. We played jump rope. Don't cry. The blood was on my shoe.

Alicia's oral telling with teacher scribing

Alicia

1. *We played at lunch.*
2. *It was in the schoolyard.*
3. *We played jump rope.*
4. *Maya fell down.*
5. *The teacher was there.*
6. *Maya was crying.*
7. *We went to the nurse.*
8. *I said don't cry.*
9. *There was blood on my shoe.*
10. *There was blood on the chair.*

Alicia's final draft with two scenes: one in the schoolyard and one in the nurse's office, plus dialogue

We played at lunch in the schoolyard. We played jump rope. Maya fell down. She was crying. The teacher was there. She said go to the nurse.

Then we went to the nurse. I said don't cry. There was lots of blood. There was blood on my shoe. There was blood on the chair.

Figure 5-2 *Alicia's writing before and after revision*

The Struggling Writer

Revision Strategies

As I wrote at length in *Making Revision Matter* (2005), we must be careful about the attitudes we bring to teaching revision. Students quickly pick up anything negative, such as the implication that their writing is bad and needs to be fixed, or that the more they revise, the more we'll make them do. Helping strugglers see that revision is a mental exercise as well as a written exercise may help. For example, let struggling writers tell you what they would do if they were to revise, *without actually having them do it*. Or suggest three possible types of revision (e.g., change a word, add a line of dialogue, add an emotion) and let them choose one to add. We can't expect students to run a marathon before they've learned to run around the block. At the same time, we must become sophisticated about revision's purpose and the many strategies for revising. It is better for a student to do one meaningful revision than none at all; it is more important that students learn to revise than to forever dig in their heels.

Here are some simple revisions that are quick enough that even the most recalcitrant writer might be willing to try one or two:

- Add a describing word.
- Add or change an action word.
- Use two describing words in a row.
- Use two describing or action words that begin with the same sound.
- Add in a sound word (onomatopoeia).
- Put an *X* in the margin of a sentence you like and be ready to say why you like it.
- Look at the beginnings of your sentences and make sure only one begins with *and* or *but*.
- Look for action words that need *-ed* added to the end.
- Find a place where a character might talk and put an *X* there; tell a partner what the character might say.

- Add in the weather, season, or time of day.

- Add in one item of clothing the character was wearing.

- Tell the reader one thing about how the character looks (curly hair, big glasses).

- Add a speech bubble to your drawing (if you have one).

- On an index card write one sentence you could add, and staple it to the draft.

The above list is not exhaustive, and it will rarely produce deep revision. However, for strugglers, the simplest, easiest revisions show them that revising is not as painful as they think. The first step is to get them to try it! See Figure 5-3 for examples of student revisions.

Of course, we hope they will move on to meatier revisions with time. Remember that they are more likely to do this if revising does not feel like a punishment. Avoid making students recopy their work. If you need writing for a bulletin board, ask students to write three revisions they'd make on index cards and clip them to the sides of the papers to display. Students may also write a reflection on an index card to clip to their final draft, explaining what they would do if they were going to revise more. They might also indicate what they are proud of in the piece, their most daring revision, what they learned by writing this piece, or what they think they will try next time. Eliciting these responses from students sends the message that the process of learning is more important than the one piece of writing they produce each time.

Living Like a Reviser

Revision is a natural part of life, whether we realize it or not (Angelillo, 2005a). We all revise every day—our clothing, relationships, entertainment preferences, favorite songs, foods, and so on. We do it easily or resisting all the way, but we do it. Trust me, I don't wear miniskirts anymore.

Student adds describing words to writing:

> Petey
>
> M&Ms are the best candy. I eat them every day in my lunch. The colors are fun and they make noise when you bite them. If I was in the jungle on survivor I would eat M&Ms all the time.
>
> M&Ms are the best <u>chocolate</u> candy. I eat them every day in my lunch. The <u>blue and yellow</u> ones are fun and they make noise when you bite them. If I was in the jungle on survivor I would eat M&Ms all the time.

Student changes or adds an action word:

> Petey
>
> M&Ms are the best chocolate candy. I eat them every day in my lunch. The blue and yellow ones are fun and they <u>crunch</u> when you bite them. If I was in the jungle on survivor I would eat M&Ms all the time.

Student adds two describing words in a row:

> Petey
>
> M&Ms are the best <u>tiny</u> chocolate candy. I eat them every day in my lunch. The blue and yellow ones are fun and they crunch when you bite them. If I was in the jungle on survivor I would eat M&Ms all the time.

(continued on page 90)

Student adds two describing or action words that begin with the same sound:

Petey

M&Ms are the best tiny chocolate candy. I eat them every day in my lunch. The blue and yellow ones are fun and they <u>crackle</u> and crunch when you bite them. If I was in the jungle on survivor I would eat M&Ms all the time.

Student adds onomatopoeia:

Petey

M&Ms are the best tiny chocolate candy. I eat them every day in my lunch. The blue and yellow ones are fun and they crackle and crunch when you bite them. <u>Crack, crack, crack</u>! If I was in the jungle on survivor I would eat M&Ms all the time. <u>Slurp</u>!

Another student adds an *X* where she would like to add a sentence:

Brittany

In the summer I am going to see my aunt in Ecuador. My aunt and my cousins live on a farm. We drink milk from the goats and play on the road. <u>X</u> I love to go there.

A student tries to begin only one sentence with *and* or *but*:

Carlos

We have a party for the 4th of July. My mother and my brother are there and my dad comes with his new car. After we eat we have hot dogs and potato salad. Then we play tag and go swimming but my mother won't go swimming with us. Then we see the parade. And then we watch the fireworks but my brother falls asleep because he is only four.

(continued on page 91)

A student checks for action words that need *-d* or *-ed* on the end:

> Andrew
>
> I like to go skateboarding after school. Yesterday I skated to the mall and my friend Mikey was there.

A student adds in one thing about a character's looks:

> Marisa
>
> My sister is really mean and she steals my toys and my clothes. Sometimes I want to hit her or pull her ponytail.

To my mind, the best way to teach students to revise their writing is to show them that they are revisers already; that is, they already know how to assess and change something when the need arises. For example, fall comes, and they don jackets and coats; winter brings boots and gloves. In summer they eat ice cream and ices to cool off; in winter, hot soup and hot chocolate. They outgrow clothing and need bigger shoes; they cut their hair when it hangs in their eyes; they squint and discover they need glasses; they find a new best friend. Students revise aspects of their lives many times in the course of a year, and sometimes revisions are foisted upon them, as when a family decides to move. Revision is a way of life, not a chore. Talking about revision all the time in this way makes it seem natural when students must do it in writing.

Now, talking about revision this way will make it seem familiar, but it will probably be no more inviting to the struggler. Nevertheless, we can count

Students revise aspects of their lives many times in the course of a year, and sometimes revisions are foisted upon them, as when a family decides to move. Revision is a way of life, not a chore. Talking about revision all the time in this way makes it seem natural when students must do it in writing.

on the habits of daily living to support us when we say that writing must be revised, just as video games and sports are revised (Gee, 2007).

Sammy is in third grade and doesn't want to revise his writing. His teacher tells me that he tries to write "perfectly" the first time, with the assumption that he won't have to revise. As a result, he writes slowly and cautiously, taking few risks with new words or interesting punctuation. If he can't spell a word, he chooses another one. His sentences are short and clipped. He presses hard on his pencil and carefully makes his letters. When he is done, he has produced his best effort, or at least the best he is willing to do. While he may not seem like a struggling writer, this refusal to understand that learning can be messy inhibits his growth. His teacher and I feel that developing a revision habit is important for his overall learning. (See more on perfection in Chapter 6.)

Another revision point we should consider is revising the units of study that many districts have instituted as part of their curriculum. These units often focus only on genre writing, while they should include process units of study as well. For example, it is helpful for students to learn about revising in a "revision unit of study." In fact, each part of the process deserves a unit of study! This means spending a week or two studying how to nurture an idea, how to proofread, and so on. In this type of study, students focus solely on a discrete part of the process, rather than looking at the writing piece they must produce by the end of the study. It makes good sense to sprinkle these studies throughout the year, especially during times when a six-week-long focus may not work. I recommend short studies on process during Thanksgiving week, during testing, and at the end of other units when there are too few days before a long break to begin a new unit.

Barry Lane tells us in his wonderful book *After THE END* (1993), "I began to realize that to teach writing, teachers must continually find new ways of revising their teaching, so that they teach an enthusiasm for innovation and constant revision that all writers share along with their ideas." (p. 13)

The Struggling Writer

- Develop a positive attitude toward revising everything in life; do not make students believe it's bad and they have to "fix it up."
- Encourage revision on drafts in folders—let students go back to previous writing to add or change pictures, words, or punctuation.
- Demonstrate revision in shared writing.
- Talk about what writers might learn from a shared read or read-aloud book that they could try in their own writing.
- Include revision strategies such as organization of print on the page, format/font, use of color, adding to pictures, changing words, speech bubbles, adding pages to a "book," changing genre (e.g., make nonfiction into a poem), and adding to a story.
- Keep a revision chart in the room as you teach strategies.
- Ask students to make at least one revision to any published piece—even a tiny revision.
- Talk about revision all the time; ask students about what they are thinking about revision when you confer.
- Ask students to write on a sticky note what they might revise if they ever went back to a published piece.
- Make revision part of reflection at the end of a study ("What would I revise if I had more time?").
- Choose a mentor author (e.g., Donald Crews, Mem Fox, Vera B. Williams, Sandra Cisneros, Kevin Henkes) for the class and point out what they could learn from the author. Ask students to try these techniques regularly and tell you when they've made revisions based on an author's work.
- Ask them to make up revision strategies for routines in the class or for other rituals in the room—let them live with revision.
- Help students establish good revision habits, such as rereading what they've written, going back to see what they can add/make clearer, living with an expectation of revision, and talking about how they revise their lives (e.g., yesterday I learned to rollerblade, I got a haircut, I helped my grandma cook for the first time, etc.).

▲ Figure 5-4 *How to help students learn to revise*

Summary

Today we know that for children to write well they must learn the writing process. Teaching youngsters to develop a willingness to wrestle with their written work until it says just what they want it to say will short-circuit the tendency to leave their writing as it is when they first write it. Careful planning of revision teaching, along with conferring to support strugglers and make the teaching specific for them, will encourage even reluctant writers to do more with their writing.

To-do list for teachers:

- Keep a notebook and practice writing to understand the process from the inside out.
- Focus on teaching process as well as genre.
- Teach struggling writers small changes they can make to improve their writing.
- Consider allowing students to use colored pencils and markers to indicate changes they want to make.
- Include revision strategies such as changes to the organization of print on the page, format/font, use of color, additions to pictures, word choices that make writing more vivid and visual, speech bubbles, addition of pages to a "book," change in genre (e.g., make nonfiction into a poem), and extensions to a story.

6

"Can I change my topic?"

Struggling With Deadlines and Expectations of Perfection

This is a classic tale. It's the day before the class's celebration of their feature articles, after four weeks of study and writing. The teacher finds Chris with his head down on his desk during writing time. When she sits beside him, he looks up with a frown.

"Can I change my topic?" he whines.

His teacher sighs and shakes her head. "Chris, your topic is wonderful. You know so much about the *Titanic*. You wrote a lot, and you did everything I asked you to do in our conferences. Why do you want to abandon your topic now?"

"I don't know. I just do."

Fortunately, Chris has written enough that his teacher is able to convince him to publish his writing without a few final touches she had hoped for, like an author's page, a "fun facts" box, and a subtitle. These last few requirements are what made Chris decide to abort his writing. He's struggling with these last bits, so he wants to postpone the inevitable. If he changes his topic now, not only will he miss the celebration and the deadline, but he'll have to face the same requirements again after writing a new article. He is not thinking ahead, but then, most third graders live in the moment.

Many students do this. They choose to postpone the inevitable, or they are unwilling to break through their difficulty with the last few parts of writing. So they just give up, even though some of them truly like their topics. On the other hand, for students who do not really like their topics, it is genuinely difficult to work through to the end. And if they are troubled by the need for their writing to "look beautiful," it may just seem like too much work for them. Sometimes they have grown tired of the topic or of the extensive work in a unit of study.

Think of a time when you had to take a required course in which you had little interest; it was probably torturous just to get through it, and writing the term paper made you feel as though you were living the great sportswriter Red Smith's famous quote, "There's nothing to writing. All you do is sit down at a typewriter and open a vein." We can understand why students procrastinate and anguish over their writing—we've done it ourselves. It's the price of doing good work in a print-driven world. Our job is to help them get beyond this. This chapter will focus on the following:

- Helping students commit to and stay with their topics
- Instituting the short publication cycle
- Overcoming the fear of or need for perfection
- Teaching students to dig deeply into a topic to find "unique knowledge"

Helping Students Commit to and Stay With Their Topics

I love to go shopping with my friend because, as a shopper, she is so unlike me. I am not a mall person at all, and I tend to buy whatever is on sale or on the first rack near the door. Done, and I'm out of the store. She tries on multiple clothes in multiple sizes and colors, asking me, "How do I look in this? Does this make me look fat? Do you think this goes with my hair?" In the end, she usually walks out with nothing. She can't make a decision and the whole event results in a feeling of overload. There are just too many choices.

We often create the same situation for young writers. Yes, there are so many topics from which to choose, and they have the freedom to go with the striped red silk shirt or the basic black scoop-neck tunic. But they don't know "what looks good on them," so they continue to try on topics long after they should have made a commitment. With so much choice, they end up walking out of the store with nothing.

It seems that for some students, limitless possibilities make them work harder. They never know if there's a better (read: easier) topic right around the corner. So they try this one and that, hoping to find one that will not only grab their attention but will also give them lots of information to write about. Even the most interesting topic may produce difficulty in finding details or significance. A topic that seems so promising one day may produce a bellyache the next. When the going gets hard, the faint-hearted writers bail out. I know the feeling—when I get muscle aches from a new exercise, I tend to give it up. It hurts too much to work through it.

By the way, the above problem may not be limited to the students in your room who usually struggle. Even your strongest writers may struggle with commitment. These students may fear that their topic won't be the best they could find, so they continually cast about for new topics. In this way, true strugglers and those searching for topics are equal.

Perhaps we need to strike a balance in writing workshop with regard to topics. Sometimes students may need guidance, particularly in matching a topic to a genre study. For example, a student may love video games but may find it difficult to turn that into a memoir. In principle, I believe any topic can fit into any genre or be a vehicle for studying an aspect of the writing process, such as finding importance or revising. But we must recognize that some topics may be too sophisticated for some students. We needn't push them beyond their abilities. It is just as foolhardy to set the bar too high as it is to set it too low.

Michaela is a third grader. She is writing a personal narrative about going to the beach with her grandmother. She has some lovely details (see Figure 6-1, p. 99) and is ready to revise when I sit to confer with her.

Janet: Hi, Michaela. Tell me how your writing work is going today.

Michaela: I don't know. I don't like my story.

Janet:	Okay, how can I help you to like it more?
Michaela:	[shrugs] I just want to write about something else.
Janet:	Gee, you're already up to revising, and you've done so much writing already.
Michaela:	I don't care.
Janet:	Hmm, I'm sorry to hear that. But before you chuck this story, let's try something. Let's figure out how to revise this story quickly so you can be done with it, and then you can write about something else.
Michaela:	No. I want to change my topic.
Janet:	Okay, let's try my suggestion, and if it doesn't work we'll talk about changing your topic. One thing that writers do when they are not sure if they like their writing is they think of an author whose writing they like. Then they do at least one thing to make their own writing more like that author's writing. Do you have an author you like to study?
Michaela:	No.
Janet:	Well, I know your class studied Kevin Henkes in an author study this year, so let's look at his writing because it will be familiar to you. (I get a copy of *Lilly's Purple Plastic Purse*.) You know, when I look at this book, the first thing I see is that it's about an object that is important to the main character, Lilly. Is there an object that is important to you at the beach?
Michaela:	Well, my pail and shovel, but that's two things.
Janet:	That's fine. Let's find a place where you can add in that you brought your pail and shovel to the beach.
Michaela:	Can I just add it to my picture?
Janet:	Well, for now, let's say you'll add it to your picture, and maybe another day you'll add it to your writing. But I notice something else Henkes does, which is he tells us the color of Lilly's purse. So what you could do, as a writer like Kevin Henkes, is go through your writing and find at least two places where you can add a color in. Let's do one together now.

Figure 6-1 *Michaela adds color words to her writing*

First try:

> ### The Beach
>
> I go to the beach with my grandma. I wear my bathing suit. I have a pail and shovel. We dig in the sand.

Second try:

> ### The Beach
>
> When I go to the beach with my grandma, I wear my yellow bathing suit. I have a pail and shovel. We dig in the sand.

Final draft:

> ### The Beach
>
> When I go to the beach with my grandma, I wear my yellow bathing suit. I have a red pail and a blue shovel. We dig in the white sand.

Michaela: Well . . . my bathing suit is yellow.

Janet: Okay, that's good. Now add in the word *yellow* before *bathing suit* all through your writing. Then find another place where you can use a color.

Michaela: Like the sky?

Janet: Yes, the sky. Or your grandmother's hat. Or the color of your beach towel. After you do that, you can call your writing finished.

Michaela: I can?

Janet: Yes. You will do one revision now by adding colors, and maybe someday in the future you'll do another. But it is better to do one little revision than to get rid of your writing completely.

Michaela: Well, I'll do the one revision and maybe two. Then I'll write another story?

Janet: Yes, then you can write another story, as long as you don't get rid of this one.

In this conference, I try to get Michaela to stay with her topic. She is far enough along in her writing that I want her to see that it makes little sense to abandon it. On the other hand, if she hasn't done much, I might help her to choose another topic. When we want students to stick with a topic, there are several ways to encourage them in that direction:

* Talk it out with them to show them how to stay with a topic.
* Have them work with a partner to talk it out with the intention of keeping it.
* Use a planning sheet (Figure 6-2); if they can answer YES to three of five, they should keep the topic.
* State why they want to change the topic *in writing*; they must have a reason beyond "I don't like it."
* Look at the class timeline and calculate the time remaining before the deadline.
* Try something a mentor author would do.
* Work through difficulty when there is something to learn from the wrestling.
* Work to build thinking endurance.
* Have nothing else waiting in the wings.
* Look at the reason for wanting to abandon: bored, tired, don't understand, can't get genre.

PLANNING SHEET: Are You Ready to Stay With Your Topic?		
My topic is something I know a lot about.	YES	NO
I can think of lots of words to describe my topic.	YES	NO
My topic is something important to me.	YES	NO
I have developed my idea in at least three ways.	YES	NO
I have talked with my partner about my topic.	YES	NO

▲ Figure 6-2 *Planning sheet for deciding whether to keep a topic*

The Struggling Writer

On the other hand, there are legitimate reasons for abandoning a topic. If we are too rigid in refusing to allow students to change, we are not modeling authentic writing. Writers do change topics, though rarely when they have done a great deal of work on a piece of writing. Still, many writers will tell you they have an "almost finished" abandoned novel asleep on their computer. Releasing a topic because it does not work is a smart decision. We must teach students the difference between "It's too hard and I don't want to do it" and "This just isn't working." (See Figure 6-3).

Students who cannot go the distance with a topic may also need to develop what's known as *conservation of constancy*, a term that refers to the ability to identify relationships and make sense of abstract information. Betty K. Garner (2007) says, ". . . they try to force information to fit into preconceived notions rather than processing to learn, create, and change. This makes abstract thinking and planning very challenging. They have difficulty transferring information from one situation to another and discerning relevance because disconnected bits of data appear to be equally important" (p. 47). Garner suggests activities for teaching constancy to youngsters, though most students learn this at home at a very young age, particularly in terms of physical measurement, such as volume, amount, length, and number. If we imagine that some students have not internalized this cognitive concept

- You don't know why you chose it.
- You have another topic ready with lots to say about it.
- You truly have nothing to say about the topic.
- You can't find information to support your topic.
- You are at the very beginning of a unit of study and time remains for you to change your topic.
- Your topic has little depth to it.
- Your topic doesn't fit the genre you are writing in.
- Your "life story" topic (see Chapter 2) would make a better piece of writing.

Figure 6-3 *Reasons for abandoning a topic*

in terms of ideas, we can see how difficult it would be to take a topic and have it meet all the requirements of writing in a genre. No wonder some students become frustrated. They may not be able to hold on to their idea and take it through the creative process, or be able to ascertain which parts of a topic are more important than others.

Aliya is a second-grade student who seems to not comprehend her teacher's questions about which part of her story is important. Aliya insists it is all important. If it weren't, she would not have written it. Her teacher and I realize that Aliya is not being resistant; she is genuinely unable to discriminate between greater and lesser facts in her thinking and writing. Another student in the class, Frank, cannot see how the topic of his dog can make an entire story. For him, "I love my dog" is all he has to say. The teacher decides that both students may benefit from work on determining importance and on seeing that all facts about a topic (e.g., my dog) can be used as part of the same story. This cognitive work eventually will help them to decide whether to keep or change their topics.

We must strike a balance when considering whether to allow students to change a topic. Do not discourage them by refusing to allow change, but do not enable them to constantly dash from one topic to the next. At most, they will have to stay with a topic for four to six weeks; it is not a permanent marriage.

Determining importance when choosing what to include when writing:

• If you could tell only one thing about your topic, what would that be?

• What are three words that tell the reader how you feel?

• Reread your notes and highlight three bits of information you know you must include.

• Reread or retell your notes and circle anything that doesn't really help the story along; then omit it from the story.

• Which signal words might you use to tell your reader to pay attention to one part of your story?

• Choose one sentence that you might write in a different font to show its importance.

The Struggling Writer

Instituting the Short Publication Cycle

Units of study (Calkins et al., 2006; Ray, 2006) are an excellent way to organize and focus teaching in writing. One minor drawback is that some teachers have developed units that last about a month each, which is quite long for some students. On the other hand, some students could use a longer time to complete the writing cycle, but not those who waste day after day in procrastination. Therefore, I encourage teachers to institute short writing cycles in addition to longer units of study. For students who lose interest in a topic quickly, this may help them to see their writing through to the end. Obviously, there will be less depth in a piece that's quickly published. Still, seeing the process from beginning to end in the space of a week or so can be satisfying for students. It can also provide a quick assessment of how well students can handle the writing process independently.

Here are some ways students can participate in a short publication cycle:

- Publish good ideas before even drafting them.
- Celebrate completing a part of the process.
- Have a quick celebration of a first draft while thinking about what revisions you might make in the future.
- Write a short piece, reusing an idea or trying a new one.
- Try an old piece of writing in a new genre.
- Write a short piece, going through each part of the process but paying attention to one part.
- Publish without your piece needing to look beautiful or perfect.
- Put the writing aside after a week, but plan to revise it in a revision unit of study later in the school year.
- Share what you have done so far: my best sentence, my favorite part, my good beginning, a funny or smart line, the strongest fact, a reflection on my writing, something new I tried, what I want my readers to know.
- Publish "what I am most proud of" in an old piece of writing.
- Publish "where I surprised myself" in your writing notebook.
- Reread notebooks and find something to publish and celebrate in an old entry.

Overcoming the Fear of or Need for Perfection

My dear colleague Isoke Titilayo Nia once told me that she had decided on a way to cure young writers of the perfection trap. With the sharp, tiny scissors she keeps in her teaching toolbox, she carefully snips off their erasers! So these little ones learn to live with and respect their own mistakes.

No doubt you've seen students who erase so often and so hard they tear through their papers. They become discouraged about writing at all because it might not look perfect. The sad fact is, some teachers and school cultures implicitly sanction this behavior by demanding that all writing be "neat" or "perfect." In these schools, nothing can be displayed unless it is error-free, as if all students in the school were perfect. Expecting perfection from eight-year-olds is beyond my compassion threshold. I am not encouraging shoddy or sauce-smeared papers, but I believe we must have common sense about what is appropriate for little hands to do. How many of us would try anything new—from cooking to speaking a foreign language—if we had to be perfect? We just don't learn that way.

For children who come to school needing to do perfect work or fearing the demand for perfection, gentle compassion is the best cure. This need can slow them down so that little writing is done. They recopy unnecessarily or they refuse to write more because they fear having to recopy it. Treating handwriting as a natural skill that all writers develop, like drawing and talking, may make it easier for some writers to practice their handwriting without becoming fearful or obsessed.

Many students come to us with this perfection syndrome as the result of a well-meaning parent or grandparent, who hopes that the child's writing will not shame them with messiness, poor spelling, and the other pitfalls that used to define "poor writing" back in the days before the writing process became part of our curriculum. Of course, those things do matter. But not at the price of refusing to develop as a writer because getting it all right is just so painful. One thing we can do for these writers is model—let them see that our writing is messy. That, on occasion, we are unsure about spelling, and we mark the word with a letter and a circle. That we go back and reread. That we draw lines through our sentences when we want to change them. And that all this is okay, for us and for them. If necessary, speak respectfully to the family about your concerns and enlist their help in overcoming the perfection syndrome in a child.

Go back to the concept of self-monitoring. Ask students how neat they think their writing must be. Do they expect their writing to be as neat as the print in a book? If so, work with them to set small goals for making their expectations realistic.

Here are some possibilities for small goals and realistic expectations:

* Make the last two lines as neat as you possibly can (or the first two, or the middle two, and so on).

* Work on one letter you want to write neatly all the way through your paper.

* Think about the words you want to use and find the spelling for them before you write.

* Do your writing on the computer!

Teaching Students to Dig Deeply Into a Topic to Find "Unique Knowledge"

A teacher once told me a story about a student in her class. They were studying immigration, and, in particular, the immigrant experience at the turn of the 20th century in New York City. The student had little interest in the subject and continually asked to go to the restroom. One day he burst back into the room after a bathroom visit and shouted, "Where did they go to the bathroom? They didn't have bathrooms, right? Where did they go? Yuck, this is disgusting!"

Being sharp as a tack, this teacher answered, "Gee, that's a great question. Why don't you find out?" Of course, she could have reprimanded him for disturbing the class or being interested in an "unseemly" topic. But she encouraged him, and he became the class expert on sewage and waste disposal (or lack of it) in New York City in the early 1900s. After his research, which included interviewing senior citizens, he had some gross and fascinating stories to tell, including accounts of the diseases caught from human and equine waste and the squalid living conditions of immigrants in those days. Perhaps he went on to be an environmental engineer!

Along with the life story, which is a personal story, a strong interest of the writer's, or a life-altering event (see Chapter 2), students may discover something in content area information that is intriguing to them. For struggling writers, this may be their entrance into writing something that excites them more than personal stories. We can support struggling writers by being aware of facts that might intrigue them, topics such as the sinking of the *Titanic*, pirates, ships and submarines, roller coasters, snakes and bears, odd or poisonous insects, medicine during the Civil War, and so on. Being an expert on something, and using it to craft several writing pieces, can be supportive for strugglers, some of whom would rather write about facts than their personal lives.

If we go back to the young fellow who was interested in waste disposal, we can imagine ways he could work this topic all year long:

- Feature article or report on waste disposal in New York City in the early 1900s
- Published interview with a senior citizen about the experience of living in squalid conditions
- Letter to mayor about trash disposal and street cleaning needs in present-day immigrant areas of city
- Piece about improving conditions for the poor in other countries
- Humorous song, rap, or poem about how much better waste management is today
- Personal narrative of a time when modern facilities were unavailable (while camping, during a blackout or airplane flight)
- Writing about reading that focuses on the theme of how difficult life was in previous centuries or how life has changed dramatically in 100 years
- Research report on how waste is processed today, including environmental concerns
- Op-ed piece about the danger of E. coli contamination from animal waste runoff in foods

The power of this angle is that it allows a student to discover an interest and mine it for many genres. Since much information is available on the Internet, students have a greater opportunity to investigate unusual topics than they did in the past. For the struggling writer, the interest may make her a star in the class, with unique deep knowledge of an unusual topic and a chance to earn the respect of her peers as an equal learner.

For the struggling writer, the interest may make her a star in the class, with unique deep knowledge of an unusual topic and a chance to earn the respect of her peers as an equal learner.

Here are some of the unusual content-area-based topics I have seen students use for their writing:

- The history of card games
- Shoes in the 19th century
- Ways people heat their homes
- Dog breeding
- How to camp in wintertime
- Native American foods
- The invention of movies
- Famines and what happens during and after them
- Awful diseases of the past
- The history of slavery
- Book binding before machines did it
- Insects and how they help or hurt humans
- Food supplies of the pioneers
- Tsunamis and earthquakes in history

Summary

Struggling writers often want to change their topics in order to avoid writing. We must recognize what makes them shiver at the thought of writing and help them get beyond it. If lack of interest in the topic is the problem, we'll help them find another one, time permitting. We'll teach them to mine a life story and also to develop unique interests in content area information. We'll establish humane expectations for neatness and perfection. And we will be honest with students when it is appropriate, or even wise, to abandon a topic. Lastly, we'll do our best to remain nonjudgmental when students struggle to stay with the topics.

To-do list for teachers:

- Choose an unlikely topic and model for students over time how you learn to work with it in various genres.

- Teach students how to decide when a topic is worth keeping or not.

- Work on determining importance every day by making connections to small and everyday events.

How to teach developing an unusual topic:

- Model that few topics are off limits, unless they are offensive to the culture of the class. (Obviously, there are some topics that are off limits in every class, for multiple reasons; you will have to decide what these are in your class.)

- Model how you play the "What if?" game in your mind to come up with a topic. (What if a tsunami hit New York? What if the pioneers all died of thirst? What if all the insects disappeared?)

- Demonstrate that this type of expansive thinking can generate ideas, but then show how to rein in an idea so it is plausible and realistic (avoiding aliens, total Armageddon, magical solutions, and so on).

- Teach students to use the Internet for research on unusual topics; teach them to be patient!

- Model how you try out a topic in several genres and how you have to tweak it to fit some genres.

- Build off student excitement and engagement; lead them to serious study by demanding facts and reflection in addition to their excitement about a topic.

- Allow students to publish their collected facts and then to write about them; this legitimizes their research work as well as their writing.

The Struggling Writer

"I lost my notebook!"

Struggling to Respect Oneself and One's Writing

In one fourth-grade classroom, writing workshop begins as soon as the students arrive. They know to put their coats in the closet, to drop their lunches in the basket, and to head to the rug with their notebooks and a pencil. But day after day, Shamika is late. While others have gathered in the meeting area, she is still unpacking her books onto her desk, digging in the pockets of her coat, and looking for a pencil on the floor. When she finally arrives at the rug, she's forgotten her notebook. A search of her desk confirms that she's either left it at home or lost it. She can't find her writing folder and her draft, and, once again, her day is off to a discouraging, frustrating start.

The question is whether Shamika struggles because she is disorganized or she is disorganized because she struggles. This is a chicken-or-egg question for most students. It might very well be that Shamika is disorganized because she truly dislikes writing. If the day began with math, she might be ready to dive right in. This is something we need to find out, because there may be other matters from her life that are affecting her schoolwork. We need to understand Shamika as a student before we can help her, for in some ways, she exemplifies what life is like for struggling writers.

Students who do not respect themselves certainly do not respect their work. It may take more than mere writing instruction to teach these students that their thinking, talking, and writing is important and deserves their respect, and everyone else's, too. Sometimes the input of other professionals in the school setting, such as a guidance counselor, will be necessary to determine how to best help a particular student.

How do we teach students self-respect? Some come to us with boisterous personalities, and they bristle at being corralled into academics. Others come with painful shyness, or as English language learners, or with a history of feeling unsuccessful in writing. We love and teach them all, but the ones who lack self-respect are the special challenges.

Start with practical matters. Students like Shamika may need to keep their writing materials in the classroom. Their writer's notebooks stay in school, as do all drafts and work in folders. If they write at home, it is on loose sheets of paper. When they bring loose work in, it is stapled into the notebook. If they lose it, there's little harm done, in the long term, that is. The teacher avoids writing notes for them on stickies, because stickies often fly away. Instead, notes are on index cards stapled into the notebook or onto the draft. Losing a notebook can mean losing several months' work. It's frustrating for the teacher and the student, and teachers often don't know what to do. Yes, they may hand the students a new, blank notebook, but the problem is that it is blank. There is no evidence of the student's writing life all year long. So do what you can to teach them both responsibility and the respect that comes from always being prepared.

The teacher may ask struggling students to sit nearby. He may schedule a daily check-in with these students or assign partners who will help them organize their work. There might be charts and outlines for them, or little red strings around their wrists. But the bottom line is that until they come to respect themselves as learners, and their writing as their hearts spilled out onto paper, they will continue to be the lost ones in the room.

We are not social workers or school psychologists, who all do excellent work in helping students improve in many situations. We are teachers, and whatever we do must be in the realm of our professional work and our training. Nevertheless, we must believe in our students, even as we teach them strategies for self-regulation and for respect.

Three recommendations for improving the self-respect of struggling writers are the core of this chapter:

- It doesn't matter what other people think of you and your writing (*you* must be happy with it).
- Writing is possibly your best chance for having a voice in the world.
- Self-respect grows when you do things to make yourself proud.

It Doesn't Matter What Other People Think of You and Your Writing

In his book *Boy Writers: Reclaiming Their Voices* (2006), Ralph Fletcher writes of the feminization of writing. Writing workshop is often taught by female teachers, who tend to value personal narrative or memoir and who avoid stories about war, video games, baseball, and other boyish pursuits. As a result, some boys feel least comfortable in writing class, because it is where they are allowed to be the least boyish. This is a wide generalization, but we do see a significant number of boys who do not wish to write because the topics they choose are not valued and they see writing as something girls do. There are several factors at play here, and one of them is "What will my buddies think?"

Indeed, what will they think? Does our insistence on sharing put some students in the odd position of having to share topics or details they would rather remain private? And what is the culture of the classroom? One year I visited a room of mostly boys, where every week they sat silently and sullenly for most of the period. We finally had a breakthrough in January, when, with shy smiles, they began to talk about their writing. This could not have happened until the teacher and I worked on building a sense of community for months, so that the boys would not "dis" each other, laugh at each other's writing, and make snide comments about writing. It was a powerful lesson for both of us: Community matters can make or break reluctant writers.

What will *they* think? I've often thought about who *they* are. My mother always said to be careful what you say because you could never know if *they* are listening. And the most pernicious for middle schoolers: If you don't have the right clothing, gadgets, friends, and hair, what will *they* think? Oh, please. It takes a long time to teach students that there are no *theys* who are important. Students have an obligation to lead their own lives with honor and integrity. Worrying about what *they* think can get them in lots of trouble! The only ones who matter are themselves, their parents or caregivers, and their teachers.

Teaching respect is establishing an ongoing atmosphere of trust and compassion for one another. It is not the result of one or more mini-lessons or units of study. It is how we respond to students, especially when they do the things that most annoy us. It is the

Student action or event	Teacher response to teach self-respect
Student rips up writing and throws it away	Teacher quietly explains that everything we write is good, though we may not realize it yet. Encourages student to keep all writing; at a later date, teacher shows student how to revise to make discarded work into an acceptable piece of writing.
Student refuses to keep notebook, or loses it	Teacher helps student determine the type of notebook that might work; provides notebook and gallon-size resealable plastic bag; kindly offers to take care of notebook by holding it in school; commiserates when notebook is lost by saying, "You must be so sad."
Student doesn't like any topic choices	Teacher encourages student to try one and respond with a short response or drawing.
Student loses draft, especially at end of unit	Teacher keeps photocopies of struggler's drafts.
Student won't/can't focus and roams room during writing	Teacher helps student find comfortable place to sit and to set small, reasonable goals.

calmness with which we offer solutions to problems and help them to work out difficulties. It is our wisdom and our trust in them, even if we think they've not yet earned it.

The Benefits of Role-Playing in Building Self-Respect

We've known for some time that role-playing can help young people learn how to respond in situations and make wise social decisions. We can use this technique to teach them how to respect their work and their writing. By allowing them to role-play in small groups or partnerships, they have a chance to explore their true feelings about themselves as writers and to gather ways to respond in various situations.

Here are some suggestions for role-playing to teach respect in writing workshop:

* How to respond when someone writes something you think is silly
* What to say when someone asks you about his writing
* How to keep control of your facial expressions when someone else is sharing his writing
* What to say after someone reads writing that is too short or too long
* How to answer when someone else disrespects your writing
* How to earn other students' trust by the way you listen to their writing
* What to say when someone has lost her writing or is searching for it
* How to help when someone has forgotten her notebook or draft . . . again

Writing Is Possibly Your Best Chance for Having a Voice in the World

Students who know that their writing goes out into the world and gets a response are better able to attach meaningful intention to writing. Therefore, you could plan for writing that goes into the local community, so that students might receive a response. You can prearrange with prospective receivers of student writing that they write back, and you can let them know via a cover letter that students are "writers in training" whose papers might contain a few errors that you hope readers will excuse. Avoid having students write to the mayor or the president or anyone else from whom they are unlikely to receive a personal reply. From a student's point of view, it is better to send a poem to a local senior citizen and get a personal reply than to write to a senator and get a form letter in return.

Early in the school year, ask students to write something about themselves that they could share with someone who is sick, lonely, or just interested in young people. It could be short and in any one of several genres. The purpose is not to go through a genre study but to produce writing that will have a real audience. This could be called "gift writing," because it is writing that is a gift to someone else. Figure 7-1 shows the genres and audiences that students might consider. Do not limit students to letter writing. A senior citizen might enjoy receiving a short memoir or poem as much as a letter. In addition, since this is not persuasive writing, there is no need to address an issue or an audience. This is an exercise in sharing their voices, and for struggling writers it can be quite powerful. Do your best to match the topic and genre to the audience. For example, a personal narrative about grandparents might best be sent to a senior center, while a story about getting stitches could go to the local hospital. The recipients of student writing are not going to grade or comment on the writing; instead, they will reply by responding with their own thinking on the topic or question. Do be careful to protect student identity by only using first names and the name of the class, in care of the school and teacher's name.

Once students have tried writing to someone in their community and have had the excitement of receiving a response, they may choose to include this option in their ongoing independent writing. The purpose is to teach them that writing is one way to be heard by others who might never hear your voice or know what you are thinking. Even a picture can be a beautiful and loving gift to a person who is ill or lonely. It is never too early to become a part of the larger community and to learn to look beyond oneself. It is as much about giving to the community as receiving from it.

> *Even a picture can be a beautiful and loving gift to a person who is ill or lonely. It is never too early to become a part of the larger community and to learn to look beyond oneself.*

Genre possibilities	Possible audiences (have recipients commit to a written response, and get parent and administration approval)
• Personal narrative • Information about student's life or interests • Poem • Memoir • Song • Story • Notebook entry (I wonder, I notice, I get excited, I fear . . .) • Extended question (several sentences about a significant question the student has, such as why money is important to adults)	• Local senior center or nursing home • Local library • Local hospital or outpatient clinic • Local houses of worship or clergy • Local businesses • Local firehouse or police station • Crossing guard, school bus driver • Community centers • Students in other local schools

Self-Respect Grows When You Do Things to Make Yourself Proud

One way to secure students' self-esteem is to teach them to be experts. Students who struggle with writing may be whizzes at science, or talented musicians, or fine athletes. We always want young people to explore and develop their talents. Some students who struggle with academic writing may not realize that they actually are talented thinkers and writers of nonacademic writing. While we certainly need to teach essay and report writing, we also should provide these students with chances to find their "writing selves."

I suggest that we consider reinstating the "open genre" study in writing workshop. (See Figure 7-3.) This study requires that the teacher be secure in his teaching, but it is one of the best opportunities for young writers to scout about and find what they would like to write. We may find that we have budding comedy writers or playwrights in our midst.

I once had a student who wanted to write a teleplay. She took this on as her independent writing all year long, and at the end of the year she actually sold her script to the producers of the TV show. Surely, this was unusual, but it showed her and her classmates that there is more to writing than preparing for tests or writing school essays.

Set aside three to four weeks for this study. If you must wait until after the statewide tests, do so. But create anticipation for it by mentioning it often to students to get them thinking about the kinds of writing that are available in the world. About two weeks before you begin the study, that is, while you are still in the revision stage of another study, begin to bring in literature of the type that students might want to emulate. Ask them to be open-minded as they search their worlds for interesting types of writing that are "outside of the box."

When a student who struggles with academic writing begins to see herself as capable in other types of writing, the effect on her self-respect is enormous. Maria is a fifth grader who has spent the first five years of school sinking deeper into her identity as a struggler. When her teacher offered a short open genre study, Maria realized that she is a "vampire romance" writer. (See Figure 7-2.) Her vampire stories are silly and funny, yet she has an audience for them, because the girls in her grade wait to read the latest one that flows from Maria's pen. They offer her ideas for the next one and pass them around. True, Maria still struggles to write science reports. She still needs to work on spelling and handwriting. But she is part of the writing community, and she is proud of herself. Each of her stories is edited by a different friend. Maria feels validated and happy. Her vampire writing continued after the open study ended.

Similarly, Sam discovers that he likes to write rap songs. What he likes is the rhythm of the music and the sense that with something to say and an ability to rhyme, he can do this. Obviously, his teacher talked to him about content, and he has agreed to self-censor the songs. He has a grand time writing his songs and staging short performances. Another student, Jamie, secretly wishes to be a comic, so in the open study he writes a comedy routine consisting mainly of corny jokes that he enjoys telling. And Donna, who hopes of becoming a playwright, decides to write an episode of her favorite TV show. Felizia decides to write commercials for her favorite snack. There are endless possibilities for young writers to see themselves as something other than writers who struggle.

The Struggling Writer

Antonio was the new vampire in the hood. He had six tattoos on his arms and had his hair shaved. Except he had one streak of purple hair in the back and a skull tattoo on his forehead. Every day he was at the corner waiting when the girls came home from middle school, and he always looked at them but he was listening to his MP3 so they never talked.

Then one day Lucy went up to him and said she liked his hair, and when he smiled, his teeth were pointy. Lucy ran away scared and her friends were scared too.

Then one time, Lucy forgot her math book in her locker at school, so she went back to get it. It was 6:00 and it was dark out already and cold. She got into the school and tiptoed down to her locker. Just when she was opening the lock, she heard a scratching noise. She jumped and screamed. When the lights went out, she didn't know how to get out of the hallway.

Then someone grabbed her hand! She screamed again. It was Antonio. He looked at her with his bluish-yellow eyes and she almost fainted. "Don't bite me!" she screamed. But then he pulled her down the hallway to the door of the school.

"Wow, you saved me." Lucy said. "Something made noise and scared me."

"It was only a rat," Antonio said. "I'm not afraid of them."

"I am," Lucy said.

So Antonio opened the door to the school and he walked with Lucy to her house.

The End

Figure 7-2 Maria's vampire romance

> - Joke writing or comedy routine
> - Graphic novels
> - Newspaper comics
> - Vampire stories
> - Science fiction
> - Fantasy
> - Jingles, commercials, or advertisements
>
> - Sports writing
> - Headlines
> - Songs (country, rap, rock, R&B, new age)
> - One-act plays or teleplays
> - Blogging or opinion writing
> - Plan for a video game or board game

▲ Figure 7-3 *Possible genres for independent writing in open genres*

Let students be as creative as possible. Let them enjoy being themselves and finding whatever kind of writing they might enjoy. This cannot, and never will, replace the academic writing we must teach students in schools, but it may give strugglers—and all students—a vision of what writing can be in their lives. Knowing that they can write whatever they want can build the self-respect that all experts have.

Summary

Self-monitoring is shown to be most helpful for students who struggle (Collins, 1998); even Reading Recovery teaches this to little ones in reading. While getting students to monitor their work habits is important, it is also possible to teach them to monitor their affect, their readiness, and their endurance, three of the assessment points in Chapter 9. Students can begin to see that there is a connection between experiencing success and pride and doing certain things in social and academic situations.

We teach self-respect when we teach students how to treat one another and how to respond to others. For example, students must know how to disagree with dignity, because this allows them to be true to their feelings without offending others. Similarly, they must know how to accept disagreement without anger or offense, for everyone has a right to his opinion, though not to hurt others.

I like to teach students to listen to the intent of what someone says, or the "music" under their words. A person can say "I love you" in ways that range from sarcastic to gentle to heartfelt. Students who can hear the music behind the words that others say can often tell if a person is being sincere or not. So one point is for students to be able to accurately identify the intent of others' comments. After that, they need to know appropriate ways to respond, even if having self-respect means they sometimes just walk away. This applies to any situation, as well as responses they might get from others about their writing.

Building self-respect is ongoing work for us all. There is much that youngsters must deal with in our world. We must do whatever we can to bolster their belief that they have skills and talents that are valid and useful.

To-do list for teachers:

- Observe all students and determine what you might want to model so that they can build respect for one another and self-respect.

- Treat all student work with respect, even when it is handed in with grease marks and dirt.

- Be careful to monitor your responses to students, including your tone of voice and your facial expressions. These tell students more than our words do.

- Find ways to incorporate independent writing that allows all students to find and develop their talents and strengths.

Part II

What Teachers Need to Know
About Struggling Writers

In these days of data and hard research, we sometimes have to remind ourselves that we work with children, not laboratory specimens. Many of them arrive at school filled with hope and childlike joy, yet some come to us sad and sullen. They live lives of great privilege and/or unbearable sorrow, and they are all ours to teach for a year or two, if we're lucky. We've entered this work because we have hope that we can awaken curiosity and model the thinker's life for them; we smile and laugh, and yet sometimes we're left with tears and frowns.

Our school communities are small versions of the bigger communities of our lives. In our out-of-school communities, we know people who are kind and caring, those who are abrasive and self-centered, and those who are needy, ill, poor, and lonely. In caring for them, we all become stronger, because our communities are knit together with all of our joys and sorrows.

What this means is that teaching is a great joy and, just as often, a great struggle. It is not a "show up and close the door" kind of job; there are no "hold my calls" kind of days. We who are called to this work dive in headfirst, exhilarated by the challenge. Nevertheless, we sometimes struggle. I suggest that the students who struggle in any area, but particularly in writing, are the ones who teach us how to be great teachers.

What we need to know about struggling writers is how to teach them. We need to talk to them with respect and to help them with love and patience. Most of all, we need to view struggling writers as mirrors of ourselves. We all struggle with something—cooking, relationships, faith, getting up on time, whatever. To the degree that we dig inside to understand ourselves, we will begin to understand our struggling students. And that is the journey and the promise of the walk in someone else's shoes.

8

Why Young Writers Struggle and Why Teachers Struggle to Teach Them

I sit here in my tiny office. Even though there is little to distract me, I think of all the things I would rather be doing than staring at the computer screen. I could take the dog for a walk. I could clean the snow off the walkway. I could call up an ailing friend, take advantage of sales at the mall, or clean out the pantry. I could finish knitting that sweater, practice the piano, or answer some letters. Fill the bird feeder, send away for vegetable seeds, empty the litter box . . . I can easily think of 50 things I'd rather be doing than writing, and I love to write. Well, to be honest, I love to have written. As satisfying as it can be, the work of writing can be tiring, frustrating, and akin to mentally giving birth. I need a nap just thinking of it.

Every day across the country, youngsters are asked to write. I wonder how many of them feel the way I sometimes do? How many of them brim with enthusiasm? More likely, they dread the experience. This is not because writing is a bad thing—no, it is one of the best ways we can stretch our minds to solve problems, communicate ideas, create significance, and learn the process of creating something just from our thinking. Writing is a paradoxical mixture of creation and struggle. It's very much like life.

Writing is a paradoxical mixture of creation and struggle. It's very much like life.

Like life, writing is both exhilarating and difficult. We do all we can to make writing fun, and sometimes it *is* fun. But like life, sometimes it's just plain hard work. We need the balance of both fun and hard work, because students who do not know the excitement of hard play and hard work will not experience the satisfaction that both can bring.

I believe one reason students resist or struggle with writing has to do with their energy level. Our culture is built around gadgets and toys that play and work—and even think—for us. I have only to program the coffee maker and there's fresh coffee at 5 a.m. when I get up. My washing machine has more functions and gives me more information than I need. My cell phone is so "alive" it frightens me. Even writing this book is easier than it would have been 20 years ago, when I wrote everything by hand on yellow sheets and then typed it on an old electric typewriter! These days, I find myself getting lazy and annoyed when asked to do things by hand that I routinely did that way a few years ago. For youngsters, writing requires more independence and energy than they are used to giving a project. They get weighed down by inertia. They look for shortcuts for getting work done. I understand this. For me, homemade soup is history; these days I microwave a mean hot dog.

Of course, there are many more reasons for writing struggles. Students have difficulty with handwriting and spelling, with engaging assigned topics or generating their own, with understanding abstract concepts, like structure and voice. They find punctuation and grammar too dry, they have little stamina for writing, or they just don't care about writing well. They think it's boring, or they've learned it's punitive. The amount they produce is never enough, and they feel defeated before they start. So many factors can stand in the way of good writing.

Yet our current culture is not the sole cause. Today we expect students to write more than they ever did, but many people have been traumatized by writing instruction over the last century and have vowed never to write another word. Writing problems have always existed. We have to stop blaming students for their difficulties and just teach them.

Before we take a look at some actual resistant writers (all with pseudonyms), let's examine what several educators recommend to help students who struggle with writing:

- Teaching self-regulation techniques
- Mobilizing the learning community
- Utilizing best practices in writing workshop

Teaching Self-Regulation Techniques

Much of the work on teaching struggling writers has centered on their difficulty carrying through on their writing. Various factors cause them to short-circuit, including becoming overwhelmed by the entire task and being unable to break a writing task into smaller parts. While becoming familiar with the writing process may help these students, some educators believe the process, as it is taught in schools these days, requires a high degree of self-regulation, cognitive effort, and attentional control (Lienemann, Graham, Leader-Janssen, & Reid, 2006; Graham & Harris, 2003). These educators advocate teaching self-regulation techniques that assist students with planning and executing their writing.

Self-regulated strategy development (Graham & Harris, 2003), or SRSD, involves teaching students explicit strategies for accomplishing writing tasks. These may include writing in a specific genre or developing control over the writing process, as well as skills and knowledge needed to use the strategies (Lienemann et al., 2006). For example, teaching students explicit strategies in writing can be more effective for struggling writers than just providing time to write (Graham & Perin, 2007). Most classroom teachers now provide daily explicit instruction in writing for the whole class (Angelillo, 2008b), for small groups, and for individuals (Anderson, 2000).

time management		note taking	
backward planning on calendar from due date to current date		choose and agree upon expected number of notes to be taken from text	
set time goals for each chunk of assignment		talk to partner to explain notes and retell them in your own words	

Much of the research indicates that writing instruction must be clear, strategic, and precise. This helps students who have difficulty managing all the discrete tasks of writing, as well as non-strugglers, to become independent. SRSD can be beneficial in helping students with generating ideas, making their way through the process, managing time, understanding genres, taking notes, and so on. For many strugglers, the difficulty lies in processing the requirements of a task, planning out their use of time, and executing their plans. These are lifelong skills students need to succeed in any area of study or endeavor. Let's look at some of the self-monitoring strategies we can teach, keeping in mind that students must agree to the strategies we suggest.

Starting with a small number of steps is a good way to begin fostering a student's ability to self-monitor. (See above for an example.) He can easily manage two tasks on his own. Gradually, teachers can increase the number of self-regulating strategies to include work done in school and work to be done at home. Once students feel comfortable with one category of strategies, teach another one, depending on students' needs. Obviously, not all students will need the same self-regulating strategies. It is equally important to note that students must understand the reason for the strategy and they must monitor themselves as they accomplish each one. It makes little sense for self-monitoring to be imposed and enforced by the teacher. Instead, teachers should model and teach self-monitoring throughout the day. For example, teachers might show students that they can ask themselves the following: When do I get tired? What makes me get distracted? What makes me get sloppy or silly? And so on.

The strategies that follow have proven effective in helping students to monitor their own writing:

- Managing time; outlining long-term goals
- Choosing and using a topic
- Building stamina
- Embracing the writing process
- Building social networks around writing
- Revising and editing
- Getting ready to publish

Mobilizing the Learning Community

The cutting-edge 21st-century classroom is a well-developed learning community. Students are immersed in the care and interrelationships of community work, routines and rituals, and play (Peterson, 1992). Classrooms are no longer places where students are ordered to "keep your eyes on your own paper." We need students who can work together for the good of the community, for the benefit of all learners, and for the experience of creating knowledge together. At its best, the classroom is a much more nurturing and accepting place than it was 50 years ago.

With the need for community comes the need to develop a sense of commonality among all students. This includes sharing stories from our lives, which always creates a bond among us. It includes sharing experiences—who can forget that delightful trip we took to the museum or how we cried together when the gerbil died? It includes learning how to speak to one another with respect and dignity, including the actual words respectful people use to disagree with or compliment one another. It includes sharing literature through read-aloud experiences and book clubs. And it includes respecting the unique talents of each member of the class and the commitment to support one another in growth. It does not mean there will be no disagreements, but it means disagreements will be settled with generosity and gentleness. In short, the classroom community is what we hope the world will become.

The initial responsibility for establishing a learning community falls upon the teacher, for obvious reasons. Teachers set the tone for the class by the way they use the environment and their authority to create comfort and acceptance versus tension and anger. Teachers invite students to learn together by the way the classroom furniture is arranged, by the way students are greeted in the morning (even when late for the tenth time), by the way we show each child how to do her best, and, most especially, by the way strugglers are treated with love and understanding. Access to the classroom library, to preferred seats in the meeting area, to the restroom and water fountain, and to generous classroom supplies all send a message to students: We are a community and we work together. On the other side of the spectrum, the classroom that is set up for opposition (Where's your homework? Did you forget your pencil again? You can't take a new book. No bathroom breaks until lunch . . .) becomes lost in rules and power struggles. Students tend to learn better from a teacher who is kind but firm than from a stern, sarcastic, or solemn one.

In this community, students realize that all members have talents. The teacher makes sure to discover and proclaim their academic talents and encourages them to discover and share their non-academic talents, such as dancing, swinging a baseball bat, and training a dog. They recognize that all talents are valued, not just academic talents. The student who has a way with animals may appear to lack academic talent, yet she may become a fine veterinarian one day. The student who likes to fix toys may become a fine carpenter one day. We deal with the present moment and the entire host of possibilities for each child. When students know that they are not in competition, but rather, are working in concert to build the best learning community for the benefit of all, the way they treat one another changes. Instead of becoming the jesters or pariahs of the class, strugglers are seen as equal members of the community who have other talents; they just need a little help in writing. Each of us needs a little help in something. And the entire community is responsible for assisting everyone to realize his or her full potential.

Donald Graves (2001) suggests that we "begin today as if yesterday didn't exist" (p. 42). Graves counsels us to forget the missteps of the past and to open our hearts and minds to erase the baggage of low expectations. He explains that in his own demonstration teaching for teachers, he asks that strugglers not be identified. All students are taught equally. Strugglers easily intuit that he has no preconceived notions about what they are capable of doing. Graves reports that each time he teaches all students equally, these children grow more expansive in their responses. Imagine if each day we withheld our preconceived notions about our strugglers and treated them as if they were our gifted students! Imagine how much harm is done when students must face an annoyed and nagging teacher each day.

Community building that relates specifically to writing takes time to develop and requires our best selves in the classroom. Yes, we are sometimes tired or harried or worried. But we overcome this because the community enables the kind of writing I'm describing. Therefore, we incorporate some of the following:

- Use carefully chosen literature to build community; be sure the story can create a bond among students in the class; be sure it is a text to which you can refer frequently; reread it to the class many times.

- Consider students' physical needs in terms of where they sit, restroom rules, and classroom movement: Do not require girls who wear dresses to sit on the floor (use a low bench instead); do not argue over hats or other headgear; drinking water should be a right, not a privilege, because well-hydrated brains think better!

- Short-circuit difficulty by greeting students cheerfully in the morning and ascertaining if there are any circumstances that may require extra attention; give this attention immediately.

- Notice the ease of movement in the classroom by getting down at a student's eye level: How hard is it to get to the meeting area? The water fountain? The library? How can you ease the flow of traffic in a crowded classroom to create respect for everyone's space?

- Occasionally coach strugglers so they have responses to class discussions; this keeps them from feeling marginalized and builds respect for their classmates' opinions.

- Do not call on students in anger or as a challenge.

- Do not bring students' shortcomings to the attention of other students ("Don't tell me you didn't do your homework again! I knew it! That's it! No recess for you!" Ouch . . .)

We can also consider making our classroom part of the larger community. I discuss this at length in an earlier chapter, but it is worth mentioning here. Perhaps members of the senior center would be willing to read student writing and respond; perhaps they would be willing to be interviewed by students. A local bookstore might allow a poetry reading night for your students. The local library might display student writing or post student questions to the community ("Does anyone know when the firehouse on the corner was built?" "How many people in our neighborhood have grandparents who also lived here?"). When we create a community for writing, we help students see that writing is part of being in the modern world and a way of communicating with others. We also help them see that everyone has a stake in strong writing instruction.

Utilizing Best Practices in Writing Workshop

Sometimes teachers tell me that writing workshop is inappropriate for struggling students. They claim their students can't handle the pressure, the independence, and the deadlines. They fear the students can't find ideas, finish their writing, or deal with conventions of writing. I feel awful for these teachers and their students. I believe these teachers may not understand the depth and breadth of writing workshop instruction because, for all its apparent simplicity and freedom, it is highly structured, meticulously planned, and intellectually rigorous. Writing workshop instruction that does not meet these criteria needs to be revised. Best practices in writing workshop are clear, precise, and long-lasting. What teachers may object to is the loosening of teacher control that untrained eyes may mistake as lack of "teaching." This is as far from the truth as possible. What struggling writers need is this type of rigorous, intelligent instruction; the tendency to require less from students is both tempting and unprofessional.

Writing workshop teaching requires the best from the teacher. Teachers in writing workshop must know their students well and they must know writing well. This creates a high standard for us, because many of us were not taught to write well ourselves. Fortunately, in the past decade or so, educators such as Lucy Calkins, Katie Wood Ray, Nancie Atwell, Linda Rief, and Lester Laminack have taught thousands of teachers how to study writing and use that knowledge to create meaningful and insightful instruction that is tailored to student needs. We are all grateful for their work and for the work of hundreds of school-based staff developers who have taken their ideas and brought them to thousands of classrooms.

The days of reading from the teacher's edition are long gone. The best way to teach struggling writers is to engage them in topics about which they care deeply and then teach them to write about those topics. These students are often the best thing to happen to a teacher professionally, because by teaching them, we truly learn to teach. In the following chapters, we will look at best practices for teaching in writing workshop.

Summary

Students struggle with writing for many reasons, some of which are beyond the scope of this text. For the regular education child in the regular education classroom, there may be distractions and difficulties to writing. Occasionally, a student may need additional evaluation to be sure her needs can be met in the classroom or to ascertain if she requires additional support. Nevertheless, teaching students to self-monitor their learning is an excellent strategy for teaching them how to learn. When learning communities and teachers are supportive and instruction is wise and clear, struggling writers can do their best to become writers in their own right.

To-do list for teachers:

* Teach students to manage writing through self-regulated strategy development.

* Begin early in the year to build the learning community and use it to support all students.

* Maintain professional integrity by studying the work of literacy teaching masters (reading their books or viewing their DVDs) and keeping current with professional journals.

* Carefully monitor your own struggles and how you respond to them and to the struggles of others.

9

Precise and Meaningful Assessment of Struggling Writers

Several years ago, I visited a school and met with the teachers to plan 10 days of staff development that would follow. After introducing ourselves, I asked the teachers to consider what they wanted most to study. The teachers agreed that they wanted to study struggling writers, so I asked what percentage of their students they'd identify as struggling.

"All of them," one teacher answered. "They are all strugglers."

While my immediate reaction was surprise, I now understand what she meant. Yes, all writers struggle with some part of writing; I'd guess that even professional writers have some writing Achilles' heel. We may struggle with any one of the following: spelling, typing, deadlines, verb tenses, subject-verb agreement, genre, mixed metaphors, lost purpose, weak endings, self-confidence, procrastination (that's me!), finding an audience, and so on. But these are not the strugglers to whom I refer, nor do I mean special education students. The strugglers I will address are the handful of students in almost every class who cringe at writing time, write little, sometimes misbehave during writing, and have few strategies for getting started and staying focused.

In order to teach these students with dignity and professionalism, we must assess their needs as writers. Assessment must be frequent and tied to instruction. It must focus on students' writing and all the habits that make up the writing event. Students must share in the assessment and should know the plan for helping them to improve. Carl Anderson (2005) tells us that assessment must begin with teachers who " . . . have a vision of the kind of writers they hope their students will become someday . . ." (p. 15). This angle toward assessment is unique because we usually assess writers, especially strugglers, to ascertain what they can't do. When we focus only on what is wrong, it is hard to see what is right, which often results in teaching that merely applies bandages to a student's difficulties, rather than the kind that flows from a vision of growth and an understanding of the student's potential. Once again, we must reject the deficit model of teaching for a wise and positive one.

This chapter will examine several types of meaningful assessment of student writing in the hope that assessment will become part of every teacher's toolbox and every struggling writer's school life:

- What state writing tests can't tell us
- How to use ongoing weekly assessment to identify student progress
- What to assess in writing

What State Writing Tests Can't Tell Us

Statewide writing tests can tell us a great deal about how well our instruction is working, but there is so much that these tests do not tell us about our writers that I often wonder why we spend millions of dollars on them. That question is best left to politicians and other policymakers; our work is to do our best to help students perform well on these tests, as imperfect as they may be.

The following is a list of items that I believe we need to know about our writers that statewide examinations cannot tell us. Perhaps thinking and talking about these questions will make us better writing teachers, regardless of these tests.

Statewide writing tests do not tell us the following:

- What a student's dreams are for herself as a writer
- How the student was feeling on the day of the test
- What the student cares most about
- How a teacher has made writing important to his or her students
- Whether a particular writing community supports all students
- What incremental progress students make from day to day
- Whether time constraints cause trouble for an otherwise good writer
- How well students use the writing process
- The degree to which problems with reading the test itself makes test-taking difficult
- How a student handles unstressful writing situations
- The priorities that teachers and schools emphasize for writers
- Whether students use writing to communicate to the outside world
- How student writing performance differs from day to day and what affects it

Whatever the shortcomings may be, these tests do provide some information that we can use to begin building a deep understanding of our students. For example, they give us a sense of whether students can write for an audience, write in a genre, and stay focused on a question. Nevertheless, we want to know more; we want to know each student's talents, interests, and struggles beyond the skills assessed on the yearly test. We must base our understanding on a strong, varied, ongoing plan of individual assessment. Without assessment, it is impossible to have informed teaching. And without informed teaching, our struggling writers will continue to fall behind their peers.

How to Use Ongoing Weekly Assessment to Identify Student Progress

It may sound nearly impossible, but the goal is to assess writers as frequently as possible, preferably every week. We must know students so well that we can notice and identify small changes, preferably positive ones. Like parents who can tell their child has a fever just by the look in his eyes, we need to know when our struggling students are making small gains or slipping. We don't get this information from quarterly district assessments; we get this from weekly assessment.

These weekly assessments do not need to be the same every week. In some cases, just collecting students' work and studying it is enough (see suggestions later in this chapter). Other weeks, you can observe a student's habits while she writes, or angle a conference toward assessment. There may be times to read student work with a checklist on the clipboard or interview the student about her writing practice. In all cases, compare the new information with previous notes and try to determine trends and patterns of improvement or success. Never let assessment slide because there are too many interruptions; you will soon find you have lost the heartbeat of your strugglers' learning and have to begin again.

What do we do when students are frequently absent? Obviously, it is hard to maintain momentum with students who miss one or more days of school per week. Conversations with parents may help, as might discussing the issue with the guidance counselor, but the fact is that students cannot learn if they are not in school, and struggling writers only

> *Research note:*
>
> Yetta Goodman is credited with coining the term "kid-watching." Goodman wrote over 25 years ago about the need for teachers to constantly watch students as they learn, rather than relying on testing (1985). Her work, along with that of Ken Goodman, has helped teachers deepen their understanding of assessment. For more on "Kid-watching," also see Owocki & Goodman (2002).

struggle more when the flow of instruction is interrupted. Knowing that the habit of missing school (except for illness) can become a pernicious problem, we must be courageous in intervening in every way. I once had a student in my middle school class who was chronically late and missed my first-period English class every day. One morning I showed up at his house at 7 a.m. to wake him (and his family) and to walk him to school. The embarrassment it caused made it necessary to do this only once. I do not recommend this tactic—I used it only because I knew this boy's family well and had cleared it with them first. But the point is that the word got around quickly that attendance at school was not optional, even when it's cold and rainy or hot and steamy. Years later, I met this young man in a park and he thanked me (in front of his wife!) for being a "teacher pit bull." Do everything you can to encourage students to come to school; they cannot learn if they aren't there.

What to Assess in Writing

Our goal is to assess students so that we can teach them thoroughly and thoughtfully. We want to know exactly what their struggles are, and to do so, it is helpful to think of categories of assessment. Even our fluent writers may struggle in an area of writing. For example, we all know the student who brims with ideas but brings no writing to conclusion. That is why assessment, along with conferring and small-group work (see Chapter 11), is so important. Our tendency is often to let the students who seem to "get it" work without our frequent assessment and teaching. But we must assume that many students struggle in one or more areas, so assessing their work and progress is a professional responsibility. With all that teachers must do every day, and the added stress of testing, it is understandable why some teachers focus on certain students. We must find a plan that works for teaching all students, not just the most needy. Remember: If they all came to us as expert writers, we wouldn't be needed!

Carl Anderson (2005) tells us that in order to gain a thorough sense of what students need as writers, we should assess them in three main categories: the degree to which they initiate writing, the quality of what they write (according to a list of qualities of good writing), and their writing processes. I urge you to read Anderson's book for the many details he provides on executing the above types of assessment. In particular, he names several qualities of good writing against which we can measure student work (Anderson, 2005, p. 58):

- Communicate meaning
- Use genre knowledge
- Structure their writing
- Write with detail
- Give their writing voice
- Use conventions

Many of us are familiar with the six-trait assessment model developed and recently updated by Vicki Spandel (2008), and another version of it, 6 + 1 traits, by Ruth Culham (2003). Ralph Fletcher and JoAnn Portalupi (2004) also have a list of qualities of good writing in their resource *Teaching the Qualities of Good Writing*. Since these lists are equally excellent, I suggest reading through each of them and deciding which one best fits your needs. Do not get derailed by the slight differences between these lists; they might use different language, but they all focus on what makes for good writing.

In one excellent school, P.S. 57 in East Harlem, New York, teachers took the six-traits assessment and instruction so seriously that they folded instruction and assessment of each trait into each of their units of study in writing. These students learned strategies for each of the traits and practiced them throughout the school year and across grade levels. It is delightful to think how much these young writers have learned about writing well.

Carl Anderson's intriguing suggestion that we also assess the degree to which students initiate writing sheds new light on students who resist academic or assigned writing but have their own self-designed writing lives. These students may not actually be strugglers. It might be that they are simply so uninterested in (or so advanced beyond!) classroom work that they are unable to stay with us. In this case, the teacher's work may be to validate the

The Six Traits of Writing

- Ideas
- Organization
- Voice
- Word Choice
- Sentence Fluency
- Conventions

The Struggling Writer

writing of these students and find ways to draw them back to class writing, perhaps with modifications. (In sixth grade, I wrote a "novel," but I did little else. How frustrated and angry my teacher was with me much of the time! She assumed I was a struggler, but in reality I was on another writing plane. Yes, I was uncooperative, but I had a rich, private writing life. All 163 chapters of it.)

Assessment should include the student's use of process, for we know that the writer who merely dashes off a draft with little planning and no revision or editing does not understand the power and depth of writing. Once again, Anderson encourages us to assess each step of the process: What strategies do students use to generate and develop ideas, draft and revise, edit and proofread? Difficulties with any of these steps will make students struggle at some point with their writing. Even the student who can quickly write a good draft in a personal narrative will need to know process when he must write, for example, a report or feature article. We can't allow students to fly by the seats of their pants.

Knowing and using the process for writing is a habit, like using a process in math or the scientific method. The idea is not to confine thinking, but rather to challenge it to be thorough and full. So assessing the extent to which students use the writing process is like assessing whether they understand functions in math, method in science, and document research in social studies. In a practical sense, the writing process should become second nature, just as learning to drive a car is initially fraught with rules that begin to give way to ease and art as they are internalized.

As we look at a piece of student writing, we can assess the writer's knowledge of process by asking the following questions:

- Is there evidence that the student has worked to develop an idea?
- Is there a plan for drafting? (This might include a bulleted list, an informal outline, a collection of words or phrases to use, some kind of web, and so on.)
- Are there visible revisions to the first draft?
- Has the student implemented conferring suggestions?
- Does the student edit the writing?

If the answer to any of these questions is "no," which is likely with struggling writers, the teacher might investigate further to see if this is an area of difficulty (or resistance) for the student. The teacher can then plan to confer with the student or do small-group work accordingly.

Other Areas to Assess

We've looked at assessing students' written work for qualities of good writing, their process for producing writing, and the extent to which they initiate writing or have some kind of independent writing lives. However, not all difficulties will fall into these categories, so let's consider the following. (Also see Figure 9-1, page 141.)

- *Affect:* What is the student's attitude toward writing, writing class, sharing writing with partners, following through on writing lessons and conferences, and contributing to the writing community? Does the student deliberately distract other writers or make negative comments about their writing? A student's attitude toward writing often reflects her attitude toward school, though one cannot assume that is the case for any one student.

Keeping a writer's notebook:

In school, writers' notebooks teach students to "live as writers." Professional writers as well as those who are unpublished often have some kind of note-taking system. This may mean long narratives in a leather journal or jottings and sketches on torn paper napkins. For students, the best system is to keep a notebook in which they write every day about what they notice, wonder about, remember, and so on. For struggling writers, it can be helpful to allow them to be creative about how the notebook looks. It might include sketches, pasted-in photos and graphics, and lists of words. Remember that the notebook is a way to access thinking, not a daily assignment for practicing handwriting! Also consider that most professionals have some way of keeping notes related to their work, whether they are doctors, social workers, or teachers. So teaching students to keep field notes of their thinking and writing projects is very practical and useful. See Ralph Fletcher and Aimee Buckner's work on keeping writers' notebooks..

The Struggling Writer

Types of easily accessible entries for writers' notebooks
- Memories
- Observations
- Connections
- Everyday events
- Wonderings
- Complaints
- Overheard conversations

- *Readiness:* How does this student prepare himself for writing? Does he come with ideas and possibilities, sharing them with you as he enters the room in the morning? Does he use his writer's notebook or other note-taking system to work toward writing projects? Does he comment on wishing he had written certain stories or that he could write sequels to them? Does he notice other students' writing and show an interest in reading it for ideas and sharing?

- *Endurance:* How long is this student able to continue writing without intervention by the teacher? When she tires, does she have ways to get herself writing again? Does she whine or act sleepy during class, either when beginning to write or after a short period of writing? Does she have strategies for continuing to write independently? Does she demand constant attention or daily conferences with the teacher?

Other Cognitive Skills to Assess

We can spend a great deal of time in assessment, and we often do. A teacher recently complained to me that she assessed students until the end of October, had two weeks to actually teach, and then had to assess them again. Each school district has its own policies on assessment, but regardless of the specifics, good assessment doesn't stop. Some school districts have quarterly writing assessments that mirror the statewide writing tests. This is fine, as long as teachers do not become trapped in constant testing and/or preparing for testing. When will you teach? When will you dive into deep assessment to drive instruction?

I urge you to regard assessment as the backbone of your instruction. Since writing is really about thinking and communicating one's thoughts to others, use the assessment areas listed above to give you clues as to how students think.

Other cognitive skills to assess include the following:

1. Finding an idea, wrestling with it, and developing it

2. Using background knowledge to extrapolate in writing

3. Understanding how and why to use details

4. Finding and using relevant details

5. Determining importance

6. Understanding structure, including order of events and categorizing of information

7. Understanding genre

8. Using writing to come to a new conclusion or reflection on meaning

9. Making connecting leaps between events or information

Summary

Assessment is the key to identifying and planning for wise instruction of all writers, especially struggling writers. When we approach writers with only a surface understanding of their needs and strengths, our teaching may fall flat or do more harm than good. Just as the prudent doctor gathers information before diagnosing and prescribing treatment, teachers must gather information to determine how best to teach all writers.

To-do list for teachers:

- Study required district assessments and work with data-analysis teams to glean information about students' writing lives as well as demonstrated skills.

- Use informal assessment and "kid-watching" every day.

- Take thorough notes when you confer with individuals and work with small groups and reread them frequently, looking for insights into students' writing work.

- Make a plan for conferring with students individually at least once a week.

Affect:

1. What is the student's attitude toward writing?

2. What is the student's attitude toward writing class and sharing writing with partners?

3. Does the student follow through on writing lessons and conferences?

4. Does the student make a general contribution to the writing community?

5. Does the student deliberately distract other writers or make negative comments about their writing?

Readiness:

1. How does this student prepare himself for writing?

2. Does he come with ideas and possibilities, sharing them with you as he enters the room in the morning?

3. Does he use his writer's notebook or other note-taking system to work toward writing projects?

4. Does he comment on wishing he had written certain stories or that he wants to write sequels to them?

5. Does he notice other students' writing and show an interest in reading it for ideas and sharing?

Endurance:

1. How long is this student able to continue writing without intervention by the teacher?

2. When she tires, does she have ways to get herself writing again?

3. Does she whine or act sleepy during class, either when beginning to write or after a short period of writing?

4. Does she have strategies for continuing to write independently?

5. Does she need constant attention or daily conferences with the teacher?

Figure 9-1 *Assessment list for affect, readiness, and endurance*

10

Whole-Class Teaching That Meets the Needs of Struggling Writers

At the invitation of the teacher, I visit a fourth-grade class to teach a mini-lesson on nonfiction writing. After I demonstrate what I would like the students to learn that day, I give them time for active engagement, and then tell them to go off to write. But seven— *seven!*—students stay back with me on the rug, whining, "Can you tell us that again? What do you want? I don't get it." Their eager but confused faces look up at me, and I realize something is wrong. My teaching—which I thought was clear and specific—was neither clear enough nor specific enough. If only I could do this lesson over. . . .

At times like this it is tempting to snap at students, "What don't you get? It's easy. Just go do it," but that's not very helpful. If they knew what they didn't understand, they could figure it out for themselves. It's also easy to blame them, but the truth is, our work is to teach. So the professional thing to do is turn our eyes on ourselves and study our teaching.

A scenario like this happens more often than we'd care to admit. It is one reason why teaching is such an art. We know that explicit whole-class instruction is a key element of writing workshop, because teaching writing strategies and processes makes students become better writers. However, some research shows us that struggling students may not flourish in writing workshop classrooms (Troia, Lin, Monroe, & Cohen, 2009). There is evidence that with too many choices and too little one-on-one teaching, strugglers get lost. It also appears that we tend to teach too globally when we teach sophisticated strategies for writing. A study by Glasswell (1999) found that, just as in reading, there is an ever-widening gap among young writers that seems to be exacerbated by "poor instruction and limited individual assistance" (Troia et al., 2009, p. 98). In Chapter 11, we'll look at the implications of conferring in writing, but in this chapter we'll look at teaching the whole class. The lack of precision in our lessons is what hurts struggling students' understanding, not the content of the lessons. So we are challenged to consider how we can make our whole-class teaching clearer—and provide differentiated instruction when needed—so that all students understand the concepts we teach.

In addition, one drawback researchers noted about writing workshop is that teachers often emphasize the importance of completing units of study at the expense of meaningful instruction. They tend to celebrate the completion of genre cycles rather than focusing on critical feedback on writing (Troia et al., 2009). Furthermore, struggling writers need instruction on how to set goals, monitor their progress, and evaluate their work because they do not do these things on their own and "good writing places a heavy premium on these components of self-regulation" (Troia et al., 2009, p. 99). Some writing workshop teachers spend little time helping to foster these abilities in their students.

This research has some important implications. While it does not indicate that writing workshop is inappropriate for teaching struggling writers, it does require us to consider adjustments we must make to our teaching. It also points to additional teaching that struggling writers may need in order to close the gap between them and fluent writers.

In this chapter, we will study the effect of whole-class teaching on the struggling writers in our classrooms, the ones who walk away confused by what we've taught or walk away with no idea what they're to do next. We'll look at whole-class teaching in the following ways:

* Precise whole-class teaching that targets the needs of all students

- Adaptations for struggling writers
- Ongoing instruction in self-monitoring

Precise Whole-Class Teaching That Targets the Needs of All Students

I learn the most about teaching from observing excellent teachers in action. Over the years, I have learned so much from teachers who care deeply about their students and their students' needs, and who demonstrate respect for the content of the curriculum. The power of this teaching lies in teachers' ability to isolate one teaching point, decide on the best way to convey it to the students, anticipate student difficulty and address it, and plan for support of all learners. It is a formidable task, but done well, it provides robust and fascinating instruction for young writers.

In *Teaching Essentials* (2008), Regie Routman describes this type of outstanding teaching. Regie advises us to become "experts at smartness"—that is, we must understand how students learn and align our belief systems and teaching methods with their learning. She also tells us that we must teach so that our students become independent and self-directed learners. We must monitor our teaching, do lots of front-loading to provide context for our lessons, and capitalize on shared experiences when modeling. Her emphasis on the importance of having fun is also well taken!

One critical ingredient to good whole-class teaching is to choose only one teaching point and stick to it. This is not as easy as it seems. As we're teaching, we often think of other examples to offer, or we recall something that happened to us, or we get interrupted by an announcement and we're off on a tangent. On occasion, I have even watched (and taught) lessons where there was no apparent teaching point at all. Therefore, teachers must first isolate one teaching point and then be sure it is significant enough to spend an entire lesson on. Beyond that, the lesson must do the following:

- Offer ways for students to use it in their writing

- Give them opportunities to talk about it with partners

- Help them envision it in their work

- Add it to the class menu of writing strategies

My lesson simply cannot meet these criteria if I'm adding in 14 other points or if my modeling or demonstration is not clearly matched to the teaching point.

Good teaching appears simple, but it is never simplistic. Like fine acting or musical performance, the work looks effortless because so much preparation has gone into it beforehand. We don't see how hard it is to play the violin or catch a touchdown pass because experts make it look easy. But we know they have practiced for hours and hours for days on end. So why is so much teaching unrehearsed? Many teachers appear to show up for lessons with little preparation other than knowing they want to teach "digraphs" that day. I worry that lessons are done on the fly based on something the teacher found online the night before or that another teacher gave her because it seemed "cute." This is not teaching. It's child care.

Therefore, I encourage you to rehearse your teaching. Tape your lessons and notice when or how you go astray. (PA announcements ruin my concentration!) Plan and practice each part of every lesson, giving consideration to the following aspects:

- How you will connect the lesson to prior teaching

- How you will model or demonstrate what you want students to learn

- What materials you will use and why

- How students will practice and process what you are teaching

- What ongoing assessment you will use

- What you will expect students to do during that writing class

In addition, routines must be established, and they must be understood by all. If a student enters late, he comes to the rug quietly. If the ESL teacher comes to the door, he must silently motion for a student to join him. If someone needs a pencil or a tissue, there is a supply available in the meeting area. Use signals as much as possible to minimize distractions. In one classroom I visit, the teacher is so adept at using signals, and her students so sharp at reading them, that her lesson continues no matter what happens. She even dealt with a bloody nose with calm assurance and some quick tissues, without missing a beat. Now those students know how important her lessons are!

Guiding Strugglers During Whole-Class Teaching

Begin supporting strugglers *before* you start your lesson. Remind them that writing workshop begins in three minutes: Let them go to the bathroom, gather their supplies, come to the meeting area before the others, and sit in comfortable spaces, all to avoid their feeling rushed or left out. Perhaps you might call them into a huddle and give them a brief, two-sentence preview of the lesson. Then, if their attention slips for a minute during your teaching, they will not be lost. You might want to prepare one of them at a time to be a helper, especially if you plan to model or "fishbowl" an action or conversation (see box below). Encourage them to sit close to you, and check in with them during the lesson and when they are practicing the strategy you have taught.

It's important to keep in mind that we are dealing with children. They will, and should, make mistakes or forget supplies or just have a bad day. We're all human. So hand them pencils or paper when they forget to bring them, invite them to sit next to you when they can't find a "good spot," be their partner when their partner is absent, offer suggestions when they are searching for answers but need to hear the words verbalized. And always treat all students, strugglers and skilled writers alike, with kindness and gentle patience. They will all "get it" at some point, and you will be thrilled when they do.

What's a fishbowl?

Fishbowl refers to re-creating a scene within a mini-lesson, as if the teacher is onstage and the students are watching. The teacher and an assistant (student, another teacher, etc.) demonstrate how to do something, such as how to converse with a partner about writing or how to respond in a conference. At various points in the fishbowl, the teacher will "break the fourth wall" and address the students to explain what he is doing. The teacher and assistant practice the scene in advance to be sure that their acting will accomplish what they hope to teach.

The Struggling Writer

Adaptations for Struggling Writers

Differentiated instruction (Tomlinson, 1999, 2004; Tomlinson & McTighe, 2006; Wormeli, 2007) is expected in most classrooms as part of best practices in teaching. Despite the challenges it brings, there are so many benefits to differentiating work that whole volumes have been written about it. Carol Ann Tomlinson, who has written extensively on differentiation, tells us, "We are also teachers of human beings. The essence of our job is making sure that the curriculum serves as a catalyst for powerful learning for students who, with our guidance and support, become skilled in and committed to the process of learning" (Tomlinson & McTighe, 2006, p. 39). This is both a high calling and a challenge.

Teachers have many questions and concerns about making adaptations for students in whole-class teaching. Many teachers object to the fact that "they all have to take the same test." Yes, they do. But our job is to do whatever it takes to help prepare each individual for the test. As Rick Wormeli (2006) tells us in his book of the same title, "fair isn't always equal." Some students just need more support. We must think of ways to ensure that students at all points of the learning spectrum will be nurtured intellectually by our teaching.

The second objection is that it will take too much time. Too much time to prepare? Too much time to make sure students are learning? Too much time to check? I'm not sure what the answer is to this, since we will never have enough time to do all we'd like to do. We find time for assemblies and bake sales, for field trips and dress-up days, don't we? I've even seen classes lined up at the restrooms for class bathroom time, a practice I sincerely cannot understand. Think of the many ways we misuse time every day! Invest that time in the 10 minutes it will take to modify a lesson, and you may change a life.

Adapting a lesson may be as simple as doing an "instant replay" for some students. Certain people need to hear something more than once in order to get it. I am one of them. Others like to have things written down so they can feel secure that they won't forget anything. (I also do this with my detailed calendar and long to-do lists!) Adaptations might include retelling a class experience as an illustration for a teaching point or previewing the lesson the day before with one or two students and then asking them to help you teach it to the class. Figure 10-1 examines some of the roadblocks to adaptation and provides some possible solutions.

Issues in adapting lessons	Teacher questions or objections	Answers that address these concerns
Time	Will adaptation make my lessons too long? Where will I get the time to plan adaptations? How can I teach strugglers without taking time away from the rest of the class?	Weave adaptations into your lesson through your choice of literature and examples as well as your responses to student questions. Use preparation time wisely; think hard about what strugglers need. Plan centers to address some adaptations and needs; centers must be academically rigorous, not just for fun. Meet with strugglers daily for a check-in and then twice a week regularly for group work.
Lesson content	How do I make sure all students receive rigorous teaching? How can I be sure the adaptations are valid? What constitutes appropriate adaptation of a lesson?	Do not water down teaching; make it clearer; use precise examples and accessible texts. Be sure you are teaching all students the same information, though you may change the method of delivery for some. Consider adapting amount of work required, length of time for work, due dates, and self-monitoring requirements.
Classroom management	What if strugglers take so much of my time that the rest of the class loses my attention? How can I know if strugglers are genuinely in need or just vying for attention? What if the class becomes too noisy? What if the strugglers disturb the class because they won't work?	Use a computer to create several quarter-page copies of the assigned work for strugglers to take to their seats and paste into notebooks. Trust your intuition; some strugglers may need extra encouragement some days; students who vie for attention may need coaching in self-confidence and independence. Establish a community that knows how to work together; build independence to control noise; play soft music; be sure writing work is challenging but appropriate. For strugglers, set up self-monitoring to keep work going: five minutes' writing followed by a drink, quiet for 10 minutes, then time to talk to partner. Seat strugglers at tables with students who can stay focused; find strugglers a quiet spot to write (one student used to snuggle under my desk).

(continued on page 149)

▲ Figure 10-1 *Addressing concerns about particulars of adapting lessons for strugglers*

The Struggling Writer

Use of materials	Where will I get materials for adaptation?	Requisition paper, index cards, and markers to make materials.
	I make my own charts and lesson visuals; how can I adapt these for struggling students?	Adapt teacher-made materials in terms of amount, size of writing, use of text, and wording of assignment.
	Are there published materials that can substitute for teacher-made ones?	There are few published materials that are perfect for what you need.
Ongoing assessment	How can I be sure my efforts at adaptation are truly helping students?	Collect weekly data from students to compare to previous writing work; look for small gains as well as larger understandings; keep notes on this.
	How can I be sure that other students are not overlooked?	Keep a class list on graph paper and note date when you have met with students in small groups; evaluate to see who needs a check-in soon.
		Know your class; you know which students tend to fall quietly through the cracks and which ones demand your attention.

Useful Feedback on Writing

The types of adaptations we can make are many and varied. They range from content and process to amount and length of work. Perhaps most helpful is useful feedback on writing. Struggling writers often do not know how to proceed with their writing, if their writing is "okay," how to revise or edit effectively, and so on. When we collect writing, such as writers' notebooks, and return them with nothing more than our scribbled initials or a noncommittal check mark, we are not supporting strugglers on their journey to become better writers. In fact, students may misinterpret our non-responses as dislike or disdain for their work. While many writing teachers discourage writing on students' papers because they feel it robs them of ownership, we must reconsider this for our strugglers.

Note that I am not advocating a return to the "red pen syndrome," which is not helpful for struggling writers either because it highlights what is wrong, rather than what is right. However, providing some written response can be helpful, even if it is conveyed through

(continued on p. 151)

- Seat strugglers near you during your mini-lesson and coach them as they practice what you have taught.

- Help students to name specifically what they will do in writing before they go off to work independently.

- Help students make a plan before they write.

- Establish self-monitoring checklists with each struggler and evaluate them together.

- Teach students to explore a big "life story."

- Limit the number of drafts you require.

- Be compassionate about requiring students to recopy work for display.

- Ask students to talk about what they have learned and what they now feel comfortable doing.

- Use a shared class experiences as a touchstone for explaining a lesson.

- Choose a simple, well-written mentor text and use it repeatedly.

- Use new vocabulary as you teach, but define it or offer a synonym so strugglers catch on to its meaning.

- Write assignments down for strugglers on charts or individual quarter-sheets of paper.

- Be sure you cover only one significant teaching point in each lesson.

- Connect each lesson to the previous learning of the class.

- Explain why you want students to know what it is you're teaching.

- Compliment students as listeners, thinkers, partners, planners, and problem solvers.

- Suggest bathroom breaks as needed five minutes before the writing lesson.

- Modify the amount of writing strugglers do, based on their level of stamina.

Figure 10-2 *Adaptations to implement with strugglers as needed*

The Struggling Writer

a conversation during a conference (see Chapter 11). I suggest writing your comments on a thin strip of paper that you can staple to the students' papers. This will keep you from merely correcting spelling, while providing feedback to students on what works in their writing and what needs more work.

In his fascinating study of struggling writers, James L. Collins (1998) recommends that students have collaborators. This relationship functions much the way a writer-editor relationship does. The writer writes, the editor reads and makes comments about places where the writing sings and places where it is confusing, grammatically incorrect, or dense. The writer usually takes the editor's comments seriously; after all, the editor has a talented and trained eye for good writing. Imagine if our relationships with students were more collaborative than corrective. Students would come to expect feedback on ways to improve their writing, without the punitive tone this procedure occasionally takes. On the other hand, Collins states that teachers are often so focused on process that they tend to neglect the skills that once formed the basis of writing instruction. He suggests that ". . . in place of a generic process approach, and without going back to traditional teaching of specific skills and rules . . . teach students to control their own writing processes and writing skills" (1998, p. 15). Self-regulation and self-practice of necessary skills may be helpful for some struggling writers.

I encourage you to find something positive to say about every piece of writing. Do not imagine that saying little or nothing is acceptable. Not only are we there to teach and guide students, we are also there to provide them with help for improving their writing. In the attempt to halt the old practice of "red-penning" everything students write, we have now run to the opposite side of the boat. Let's give gentle and wise instruction in response to student writing so they understand what works and what doesn't. They will not pick up writing by osmosis.

Ongoing Instruction in Self-Monitoring

We all self-monitor. It is necessary for survival as well as academic success. Some of us

- Always bring your writing and a pencil with you to school; check for them in your book bag before you go to bed at night.

- Keep your writing in a folder; keep your writers notebook in the folder, too.

- Keep a sheet of paper in your book as you read so you can jot down words you want to use in your writing.

- Repeat the assignment to yourself, your partner, or your teacher before going off to write.

- Get down to writing before getting involved with distractions; give yourself the count of 20 to be sitting with writing book open and pencil in hand, looking at the book.

- Keep a bottle of water on your desk so you can take a drink without getting out of your seat and stopping your work.

- Set a daily goal for writing; it could be three lines, as long as it is one line more than you wrote the day before.

- Stop regularly to think about your purpose and your story; reread your writing.

- Practice skills once you have finished writing for the day.

- Look back at your work and be proud of what you've done.

- Forgive yourself when you have a bad day and just go on writing.

Figure 10-3 *Self-monitoring techniques for struggling writers*

are better at it than others. Others, like me, need lists, lists, and more lists. My totally-in-control mother self-monitored with virtuosity. She did all her grocery shopping without a list and never forgot anything. She never forgot a doctor appointment or an errand such as picking up clothes at the dry cleaner. She never forgot to have dinner ready on time or to do the laundry. She was a self-monitoring master. If I don't write everything down and post it on the fridge, it won't get done. I've long ago forgiven myself for this, and I just go with the lists. I appreciate the work a good list can do for me!

Self-monitoring is bigger than just making lists and crossing items off. But it is a helpful learning strategy for struggling students, who often have trouble just remembering all they have to do in class. In the sea of the hundreds of decisions we require students to make in

The Struggling Writer

the course of a day, some students are going to need help in self-monitoring. They need to set short, achievable goals each day, they need to make plans for the day's work and long-range plans for the week, and they need the visible thrill of meeting those goals and celebrating.

For struggling writers, the self-regulation may cross many areas of study. They may need to figure out how to keep a social studies notebook, file their math homework, or remember where they put their assignment pad. Do not try to teach them more than one thing at a time, and do not put more than three items on lists for them. Until I built up my stamina, having 10 to 20 things on it was overwhelming!

Summary

All students need and deserve the best teaching possible. They deserve teaching that is clear and precise, that focuses on only one teaching point for the day, and that provides enough support so they can follow through and actually try it. Teaching points should be significant, but they also should be slightly challenging for students. Nothing bores students more than hearing something they've mastered already. As for strugglers, we assume the best of them. We offer some adaptations of our lessons, but never so much that strugglers feel left out or inferior. We create conditions where they are prompted ahead of the lesson so the lesson is familiar to them, and we offer instant replays if they need them. Finally, we consider how we can embed language and shared life experience examples into our teaching so that struggling writers can understand our lessons and feel they are part of "the literacy club" (Smith, 1988).

To-do list for teachers:

- Use time in conferring to teach students self-regulation.
- Enlist each student's help to figure out will work for them.
- Be vigilant in maintaining a soft voice and patience with all students.
- Identify one or two of your own personal struggles and use them as teaching tools.

11

Conferring and Small-Group Work for Struggling Writers

I recently met with a group of fourth- and fifth-grade teachers who were worried about their students' writing, especially in response to literature. We spoke about structures they might institute to help their students, and then I asked them about their conferring. There was silence.

"You know, I mean *conferring*, meeting one-on-one with students for individual teaching," I prodded.

More silence. Then a spokesperson for the group answered, "We don't do that. We don't have time."

I felt my head swirl as I summoned my kindest voice. "Well, that's what we'll have to work on together in order to help your students with their writing. If you don't confer with students, it will be almost impossible to move their writing forward."

There is nothing I can say to soften this assertion: Conferring is the single best teaching technique we can do for students. Period.

Carl Anderson has long been a national expert on conferring. In his most recent work on the subject, he offers us many types of conferences from which to choose (Anderson,

2009). This is brilliant work that offers teachers solutions for their conferring blues. No, conferences do not mean checking up on whether students are doing their work (though sometimes you might do that). No, conferences do not mean correcting student writing and returning it for recopying. And no, conferences are not a burden on the teacher's time, and a chance for students to "check out." Yes, conferences are the best way to get to know your students deeply as writers and to build individual writing instruction. Therefore, it follows that conferences are important for all students but essential for strugglers.

A robust plan of instruction includes three types of teaching: whole-class instruction for concepts and procedures that all class members must learn; small-group instruction for enrichment, support, or interest-driven instruction; and individual instruction, where we come to know our students as thinkers and learners as well as writers (Angelillo, 2008b). When any of these elements is weak, learning suffers. Managing these three elements should be a goal for all teachers.

In this chapter, we will look at the following ways to help struggling writers:

- Conferring as conversation
- Differentiating conference style
- Small-group work

Conferring as Conversation

Let's begin by reviewing a critical point for successful conferring: A conference is a conversation. It is also one-to-one teaching, but the teaching point grows from the conversation between two writers, much the way I chat with a friend about my writing over coffee. There's no coffee in the classroom, but the atmosphere is the same: I pull a chair next to a student and ask him to talk to me about his writing. There is trust and respect in the conference, because I show the student that I deeply care about him when I spend time conferring (Anderson, 2000). I'm most interested in what this student needs to grow as a writer, not in perfecting this one piece of writing in front of us. Don't misunderstand: I do not ignore the writing on the desk, but I use it to decide what the student needs to improve as a writer in this piece of writing as well as the next and the next. Lucy Calkins (1994) tells us, "Our decisions must be guided by 'what might help this *writer*' rather than 'what might help this *writing*'" (p. 228). We do little good if we help fix up the piece at hand, but the student has learned nothing about writing other than that the teacher can fix it up for you. In fact, Calkins tells us we may actually be doing harm if the student loses trust in himself as a thinker.

Conferences are sacred times between teacher and student. We may not be able to confer as frequently as we would like, but that does not excuse us from conferring at all. Struggling writers can learn the most in conferences, because the teaching is tailored exactly to their needs. Conferring must be taught as a classroom structure so that students learn to work independently while you confer with others. A class that is constantly calling for your attention or intervention will make conferring difficult. In this case, your work would be to figure out what to set in place to help the students respect conferring time. You might ask your administrator or a colleague for assistance, but the solution is never to abandon conferring. Students must be taught from the first day of school that conferring is not to be interrupted and that all students will have their fair share of the teacher's time and wise counsel.

Let's look at the transcript of a conference with Isaac, a struggling fifth grader. This teacher does not reteach her mini-lesson, which was about a way to gather information for a memoir. She spends time with the student to help him discover something that might be helpful to him as a writer, based on this conversation and her notes of previous conferences. Her prescription for him is something doable yet important. Writers vary the length of their sentences purposefully. This is something he can do again and again, not just in this one piece of writing.

Teacher: [sits down next to student with notebook] Hi, Isaac. Talk to me about your writing today.

Isaac: It's good. I'm writing about my dog.

Teacher: Oh that's great. Is it a notebook entry or part of your memoir?

Isaac: [shrugs] I don't know.

Teacher: Well, it looks like it's a notebook entry now, but perhaps it will grow into a memoir later on. What do you think?

Isaac: Yeah, sure.

Teacher: So what is the writing work you are trying to do today?

Isaac: Write about my dog.

Teacher: Hmm, yes. But what is the work you are trying to do as a writer when you write about your dog?

Isaac: Uh . . . tell the story?

Teacher: Okay, that's good. [looks back at conferring notes] Now, the last time we met, you were trying to tell the story of your cousin falling during a basketball game. And we said that you could pick up the pace of the story by writing a few choppy sentences right before he falls.

Isaac: Yeah, I did that.

Teacher: Yes, you put it in my basket and I read it. Good job. So, today I'm thinking we could expand that idea a little in your story about your dog. You know, sometimes we think we have to always try to write longer sentences, but having some short sentences here and there really gives the reader a rest as he reads. [looks at the dog story] I see your story is about your dog running away in the park, so perhaps you could think of a way that you could use a few short sentences here. Some writers use a character talking or a character's action.

Isaac: Well, I was yelling at her to come back.

Teacher: That's good. Could you write some dialogue that is short sentences to show how upset you were?

Isaac: Like this? "Hey! Come back! Dog! Come here!"

Teacher: Yes, that sounds great. Now all you have to do is reread your work and decide where you want to add those short bits of talking. Remember that writers use long sentences and short sentences depending on what is happening in the story. Using short bits of dialogue can let your reader know you were upset, worried, or yelling. So the work I'd like you to do today is to reread your writing and put an *X* on at least two places where you can add short lines of talking. After you finish doing that, you might want to practice doing it in another notebook entry. Okay? So now, tell me exactly what you are going to do.

The teacher in this conference knows the student well because she has had one conference per week with him since the beginning of school. It takes discipline and commitment to get to conferences and to confer with every child in the class every week. True, there are weeks when this won't happen, when class trips, assemblies, and so on interrupt the flow of the week. But these must be the exceptions rather than the rules. If you are not conferring with your students every week, examine how you are spending time. When I do this with a teacher, we often find that time is frequently misspent in various nonacademic interactions. Conferring must be the priority.

How Conferring Helps

Conferring helps struggling writers because it is specific to the needs of the writer. The teaching in a conference is directly suited to the student's work, and is strictly between the teacher and the student. It is hard for students to lose focus when the teacher is sitting right next to them and the conference only lasts five or so minutes. The teacher who uses conferring notes thoughtfully is able to build on previous conferences as well as to hold the student accountable for what was taught in those conferences. The teacher assigns specific work, often writing it down for the student, especially in lower grades, and it usually is something significant but manageable. For example, in the conference with Isaac, the teacher might ask him to share what he has learned in the conference during the sharing portion at the end of writing time (Mermelstein, 2007). He then has the opportunity to teach others what he has learned and to recognize how useful the strategy is for him and for the whole class.

Some teachers worry that, given the numbers of students in their classrooms, they will not be able to confer with everyone at each stage of the writing process. Alas, this

- Provides regular one-on-one teaching time

- Tailors instruction to students' needs instead of repeating mini-lessons

- Helps develop teacher's line of thinking about the student's learning and writing needs

- Gives students the opportunity to rehearse thinking and writing with the teacher

- Allows the teacher to assess ongoing progress and adjust instruction accordingly

- Builds bond of trust between teacher and student; builds student confidence

- Coaches and teaches in nonthreatening setting

Figure 11-1 *Ways conferring helps teachers support struggling writers*

is true. As Carl Anderson (2000) assures us, "We have to make our peace with that inevitability" (p. 166). We know that if we focus our conferences on teaching something significant about writing, students will learn something important, regardless of where they are in the process and regardless of the quality of the current piece of writing. Set goals for seeing writers regularly and do not deviate from them, and your struggling writers will no doubt improve.

Differentiating Conference Style

Conferences have a structure and a purpose. Sometimes we'll research a student's long-term needs. Other times, we know that a student needs to work on, say, revision, and each conference will focus on that. Some students will want to learn to write a certain way (for example, in the style of sports articles), and we may coach them toward that end during conferences.

Teachers also need to be thoughtful about how they schedule conferences and when to introduce or discuss particular content. We can think of conferences for strugglers in these terms:

- Process (including generating ideas and revision)

- Conventions

- Writing life (habits and routines that support writing through the day)

Some conferences will begin with a phrase, such as Carl Anderson's opening, "How's it going?" I often say, "So talk to me about your writing work today." Each of these phrases is open-ended enough that students can be free to steer the conference in any direction. However, we can also include other types of openings that focus on each of the three categories above. For example, I might begin by saying, "So talk to me about how you are getting ideas for your writing today." This nudges the student in a particular direction. I could also begin by asking opening questions or phrases such as the following:

- Last time we talked about working on some spelling strategies. How is that going for you? Show me how you've done.

- Talk to me about how you are using punctuation to help your reader understand your story.

- Tell me about some of the revision strategies you are thinking of trying in this piece.

- Tell me how you'll know when you are ready to write your draft.

- Talk to me about how you are finding time for writing at home.

- Take me on a tour of your writer's notebook and tell me how you are using it.

Each of these opening lines has a purpose. Certainly, you want to have conferences with strugglers on conventions, but if that is the *only* type of conference you have, it will quickly become a sour experience for the child. Remember that strugglers, even more than your other students, need to feel safe in conferences. Do not pile on questions or requirements, but teach with firm gentleness and high expectations for success.

- *Process conferences* focus on any part of the writing process and the strategies needed for improving in the process. This includes getting and developing ideas, using strategies for drafting, revising, and editing, and rereading for meaning and genre.

- *Conventions conferences* focus on how the student is using written conventions to make meaning in writing. This includes punctuation and grammar as well as font, placement of words on the page, and use of parts of speech.

- *Writing-life conferences* focus on ways to live as a writer. This includes keeping a writer's notebook, taking notes, collecting words, becoming curious about the world, writing outside of school, using writing across the content areas, and setting personal writing goals.

Small-Group Work

I want to reiterate that small-group work is one of the three essential types of classroom teaching. It is not a substitute for individual conferences. Even when we feel rushed and overwhelmed, small-group work cannot replace conferences. Students need and deserve both, because each has a different purpose. We may have to juggle our schedules, but remaining flexible will help us to fit in both small-group work and conferences.

Small groups usually meet for a short time for a specific purpose. In my own class, I gathered small groups together for "guided writing" whenever I noticed that several students had a similar need. In Susan's fourth-grade class, there are three students (who may not all be strugglers) who continually neglect to write endings; instead, they stop writing at the end of a page and scribble "The End." Susan decides to have them meet with her as a small group once or twice a week to explore several ways to write endings. After the students have become confident about using three to five endings, Susan disbands the group. She even schedules a short celebration so they can share what they've learned with the class. Teachers find it helpful to call together these types of groups to work on a specific goal, without forcing students to be part of one group or another for too long.

Another benefit of these small groups is that they enable teachers to reach more students in less time, but not at the expense of conferring. They simply provide a tool for teaching a few students who have a common need. As noted above, it is not appropriate to put all strugglers together in a permanent "struggling writers group," because not all writers struggle for the same reasons. It makes better instructional sense to look across the class to determine which students need support in certain writing strategies or skills. Of course, on the other end of the spectrum, you can provide enrichment in small groups; in fact, a struggling writer could be part of an enrichment group, depending on his needs. Including a student who sometimes struggles in a group that is working on enrichment can be a big confidence booster, provided you are sure the student can do the thinking work involved. Examples of this might be a group of students who want to write fantasies, another focused on sports articles, or one that wants to make posters for a social justice project.

Small-group work must be planned as carefully as mini-lessons. There should be a dedicated place (small table in the center of the room, corner of the rug, and so on) where students know that small groups meet. In addition, small groups should only take 10–15 minutes, so the students must rehearse getting to the meeting place quickly with their supplies, and the teacher must get started quickly. After a small group meets, there should be enough time left in the writing period for a few conferences.

Summary

Conferences are the key to successful teaching of all students, especially struggling writers. Learning to confer is a career-long endeavor that teachers can share with colleagues and administrators. It's critical to keep in mind that a conference is not a means for reteaching or checking up on the mini-lesson. A conference is one-on-one teaching that is tailored to a student's needs as a writer.

To-do list for teachers:

- Plan how you will fit small-group instruction into your writing time block.

- Assess student writing to determine needs; if too many students need the same lesson, it is best to teach it to the whole class.

- Be open-minded; try to mix abilities in the small groups as much as possible.

- Do not assign a struggler to every small group you convene; give these students time to process what you've taught, to practice writing, and to feel they are part of the larger class (rather than someone who always needs extra help).

Final Thoughts

I leave the study of struggling writers here, knowing there is still much to learn and much to do. Perhaps it is true that with the prevalence of electronic text, students will become better writers. Certainly, e-mail and instant and text messaging serve to increase the amount of writing they do. And while this is not academic writing, it still counts for something. To deny this is to run the risk of becoming negative and stodgy. Any writing is better than no writing at all. Let's be willing to meet them halfway in an effort to draw them into writing. And let us do our best to stand up for students against ridiculous writing requirements or assignments. If we don't do this, we risk letting some students leave our schools continuing to hate writing.

I deeply believe that there is something else we can do for them. We can offer them our good will and blessings. Yes, you read that correctly. Go ahead and pray for them. Forgive me for this, but I believe it is true. I am not suggesting any particular type of prayer, and definitely not prayer of any one religious group. In fact, even nonbelievers can pray or meditate by offering up their good will to students. I am not suggesting reinstating prayer in school, nor do I envision silent-prayer sessions with students. But a *teacher* may sit quietly at his desk before students arrive and ponder the blessing of each student. Many students—and teachers—do not have someone to support them with ongoing thoughtful intentions. Imagine if we held our strugglers in love; might it assist in bringing them goodness and success? If nothing else, this attitude of prayer might change us, for it is difficult to be harsh with someone you bless daily.

Let us remember that each of our students is there for a reason. They are not merely an endless parade of students from one year to the next, creating problems and extra work for us when they struggle with the curricula we must teach. Each one is there to teach us something. It may be something about teaching. Usually it is something about ourselves. It was the strugglers in my various classes who taught me—while I kicked and wrestled— that I needed to become more compassionate, calm, loving, patient, gentle, caring, soft-spoken, thoughtful, nonjudgmental, and positive. I am a different human being now, because of all those young faces who sat before me for all those years. I wish I could thank them all, and, sadly, apologize to a few.

In my volunteer work teaching writing in a prison, I meet men who have struggled to write their whole lives. Yet their voices are strong and their stories are heart-wrenching. They desire to communicate what burns in them, and they want to reach out with their words to warn young people of the snares awaiting them. At the risk of being simplistic, I wonder how many of these men went down a wrong path because no one saw a way to work through their writing struggles. I don't know. But I do know that many of them have found salvation and comfort in their writing. We cannot afford as a society to allow more children to fall through the writing cracks.

We see in them the mirrors of our own lives, in the ways we struggle to understand and to live every day. We all struggle with something, and some of us struggle more than others. Those who think they don't struggle aren't paying attention. Exhaustion, family duties, household chores, financial burdens, illness, personal sorrow . . . all these take their toll. Just watching the evening news can make us struggle to find hope and joy in the world. To the extent that we support struggling writers, we shield them from another burden in their lives. We cannot take away the inevitable pain that comes with being alive, but we certainly can be part of building some joy and beauty into their lives.

The Struggling Writer

Building Reflection Into Writing Workshop

Struggling students need to have time to reflect on their learning as much as anyone else. Part of making the struggle less overwhelming for them is to have them understand exactly where they struggle and where they are experiencing success. Build reflection into every day's work, as well as into weekly reviews, the end of each part of the process, and, of course, the conclusion of a unit of study. Teach students to be explicit about what they have learned and what they still need to work on. For example, you can use a version of the sheet below to have students reflect on one part of their work at a time. Feel free to revise this chart to fit your needs, though I would avoid adding grades to it.

Name:	Date:
One thing I learned about writing this week (or in this unit of study) was:	
One thing I tried to do that was new for me was:	
One thing I would like to learn to do is:	
I am really proud of the way I:	
Here is one thing I want readers of my writing to notice:	

Strategies for Helping Struggling Writers

Some general principles for teaching, especially when teaching students who struggle with or avoid writing:

* Be patient. Believe in "wait" time. Remain confident in students' abilities, even when you (and they) are discouraged. *Expect* that they have something to say and to write that is fabulous.

* Listen carefully in conferences. Wait for the one tiny gem of information they give you that clues you in to what to teach.

* Be aware of their avoidance games. Push ahead and always teach them something. Get to the other side of resistance by consistently demonstrating that you will teach them something about writing every time you meet with them.

* Be flexible. Look for creativity and originality in their thinking and new possibilities for their work.

* Monitor yourself! Be careful that you do not communicate frustration or anger through eye movement, facial expressions, or tone of voice. No head-butting! In a contest of wills, students usually win; at the very least, they can make you continually aggravated. Keep a professional demeanor, as if you were their doctor or lawyer.

Specific Teaching Strategies
for Reluctant Writers

- Allow students to try sketching as a way to stretch their thinking and as a way to get them started.

- Teach them to refer often to the word wall; make sure the word wall is current, accessible, and practical.

- Work with them to develop and use a personal word bank.

- Practice visualization in which they help *you* to visualize their story.

- Use self-regulation strategies; help students develop their own techniques for getting their work done.

- Teach purposes for organizing strategies; practice when and why to use graphic organizers.

- Use computers for keeping a writer's notebook and for all writing (if possible).

- Teach the "life story" (see Chapter 2) as a way to always have something to write about.

- Consider how blogs, text messaging, online reviews, and so on may help them build identities as writers.

- Focus on qualities of good writing in every unit of study so they have tools to improve their knowledge about how to write.

- Provide small-group work and practice in conventions; help them see conventions as tools for writing, not stumbling blocks.

- Be aware of the social ramifications of being a struggler in the class. Notice how others treat strugglers and how they respond. Make sure all learners are treated with dignity and respect.

(continued on page 168)

Specific Teaching Strategies for Reluctant Writers

- Provide simple but profound techniques to make their writing much better in a short period of time. For example, teach the sentence-fluency technique of one sentence following another in line. Teach making a list of words that begin with the same letter/sound and using it to insert alliteration into writing.

- Provide opportunities for independent writing of their choice (genre and topic); be accepting of the topics they like and teach them *how* to write within those topics.

- Plan quick, short celebrations where they can feel successful (e.g., "share one sentence or revision or punctuation usage you did that you like").

- Choose one mentor text and use it over and over with strugglers until they know it by heart. Even a simple text contains lots to teach and to learn. Students can begin to feel expert at using the text and secure in returning to it for help.

- Be flexible about how students keep writer's notebooks. Consider computer notebooks, especially when small hands hurt from writing.

- Coach them to become good oral storytellers. Use video and audiotape to let them rehearse storytelling. Organize students into storytelling groups that remain together all year so they become comfortable telling stories to the other members of the group.

- Build a repertoire of ways to extend or expand a basic story. Practice this orally at first, then on paper.

Word Study in the Reading/Writing Classroom

Word-study structures to put in place:

- Word walls for high-frequency words

- Personal spelling lists

- Wordplay in notebooks

- Vocabulary use in classroom (see Sandra Wilde's work [2007] and Isabel Beck's research [2002])

- Collecting words in notebooks and using them in conversation and writing

- Word hunts in independent reading books

- Study of conventions that signal new words in fiction and nonfiction

- Rubric additions for use of interesting words as part of the "word choice" quality of good writing

- Study of an author's word choice in author study to grow word bank and to grow sense of how writers use precise words and why

- Wordplay, such as changing the part of speech (e.g., *goat* to "goating"), conjugating as play, or composing sentences with different words to energize the meaning

- Classroom atmosphere in which words are fascinating and delightful

- Study of words in the outside world and how they influence our behavior

- Magnetic letters and whiteboards for wordplay

If You See/Hear This . . . You Can Do This . . .

If You See/Hear This . . .	You Can Do This . . .
Student has trouble adding in revision	• Teach writing the revision on an index card or sticky and stapling it to the draft • Teach oral revision, e.g., "What would you do if you were going to revise?" • Keep a revision chart and ask student to choose a strategy from it
Student exhibits lack of stamina	• Teach the process as a series of goals to celebrate • Build stamina slowly by setting short, attainable goals in terms of amount and time • Ask student how much he/she can do and ask student HOW he/she will get him/herself to do it
Student doesn't want to write or cannot stay on task	• Break up work into smaller tasks • Teach self-monitoring techniques • Give choices • Ask student to listen in to conference with other students to get ideas • Teach gathering: make lists, use bullet points to write a draft • Talk to write • Use index cards as tools to manage writing and make task appear more doable • Sketch to stretch, then write off sketch • Offer four days of work + one day choice
Student wants to work with someone else, but becomes social	• Student must earn the time • Devise exit ticket • Manage time with specific task and timer for amount of time • Build in time for partner talk and work regularly; make this work focused; require check-ins
Student repeats language of the mini-lesson (teacher-pleasing), but does not appear to understand or doesn't follow through	• Take one item the student says and ask for evidence of how it can help in the writing • Ask student to refer back to recent (or long-ago) mini-lessons • Ask student to explain in his/her own words and point to it in writing • Ask student to teach it to someone else (be an expert) as you observe

(continued on page 171)

The Struggling Writer

Student doesn't apply mini-lessons to independent work on a regular basis	• Determine the student's level of independence; offer choice of selected mini-lessons • Coach student to self-monitor with self-praise • Expect work in smaller chunks • Coach student to use class charts to revisit mini-lessons • Offer variation of mini-lesson • Teach the student to get started "on the rug" before he or she loses the point of the mini-lesson
Student lacks energy and confidence	• Help the student get started • Build confidence by making him/her an expert in something • Focus on self-selected topics that are high-interest
Student changes topics frequently	• Provide rubric for deciding if topic is worth pursuing • Set deadlines for changing topics • Require the student to complete all pieces—emphasize that there is something to be learned from every piece of writing • Talk and write about what went wrong; make this specific so the student can repair and continue • Demonstrate that choosing a topic is a commitment of only a few weeks, not forever • Teach the "life story" as a way to mine one topic for a long time
Student has too many ideas and cannot choose one	• Give the opportunity to write all topics through various genres • Plan out independent writing projects with student so that all topics will have a chance • Set criteria for robust topic choice to help narrow down
Student doesn't answer in conferences	• Wait with a smile and gentle confidence in student—be patient—and usually student will fill the silence • Model writing whatever comes to mind • Model sketch to stretch thinking • Teach having intentions for writing • Teach closing one's eyes and picturing; make this explicit

(continued on page 172)

Student is able to tell a good story verbally but cannot/will not write it	• Teach story mapping • Take notes as student talks and give as a gift • Audiotape the story, then write • Share the pencil • Try changing tools (fancy pen, teacher's clipboard, novelty paper, etc.) • Help student to fulfill writer's needs—location, lighting, total quiet or soft music • Teach computer skills
Student appears distracted	• Teach students to be aware that they are distracted, i.e., what it feels like or how to catch yourself getting distracted • Note that sometimes it's okay to get distracted, but to count to 10 and refocus • Teach students to learn what triggers distraction for them; then practice getting beyond the distraction, whether it is noise, movement, or something else • Anxiety can lead to distraction, so have students breathe deeply, drink water, walk around the room once, find a comfort zone in the room, stretch, then get back to work • To make this concrete, teacher can respectfully or humorously model what daydreaming, distraction, or mind wandering looks like
Student has trouble visualizing his/her writing	• Talk about, then write using senses • Stop and sketch to help recall • Make a mental picture, then revise it • Try playing soft, ambient music • Tell stories with wordless picture books • Practice with role playing, improvisation, miming, or tableau
Student avoids writing because of spelling	• Establish spelling study, especially with patterns (see Wilde, 2007) • Reassure student that writers mark "sp" when they can't spell a word—rereading writing immediately afterward to work on correcting spelling • Establish personal spelling lists
Student avoids writing because of handwriting	• Get a computer ASAP! • Allow for some handwriting practice akin to art or calligraphy • Look at photos of illuminated manuscripts and talk about care and art • Slow writing down • Use icons to remember what the word is

References

Anderson, C. (2000). *How's it going? A practical guide to conferring with student writers*. Portsmouth, NH: Heinemann.

Anderson, C. (2005). *Assessing writers*. Portsmouth, NH: Heinemann.

Anderson, C. (2009). *Strategic writing conferences: Smart conversations that move young writers forward*. Portsmouth, NH: Heinemann.

Angelillo, J. (2002). *A fresh approach to teaching punctuation: Helping young writers use conventions with precision and purpose*. New York: Scholastic.

Angelillo, J. (2005a). *Making revision matter: Strategies for guiding students to focus, organize, and strengthen their writing independently*. New York: Scholastic.

Angelillo, J. (2005b). *Writing to the prompt: When students don't have a choice*. Portsmouth, NH: Heinemann.

Angelillo, J. (2008a). *Grammar study: Helping students get what grammar is and how it works*. New York: Scholastic.

Angelillo, J. (2008b). *Whole-class teaching: Minilessons and more*. Portsmouth, NH: Heinemann.

Beck, I., Kucan, L., & McKeown, M. G. (2002). *Bringing words to life: Robust vocabulary instruction*. New York: Guilford.

Buckner, A. (2005). *Notebook know-how: Strategies for the writer's notebook*. Portland, ME: Stenhouse.

Calkins, L. M. (1994). *The art of teaching writing* (2nd ed.). Portsmouth, NH: Heinemann.

Calkins, L., Chiarella, M., Cruz, M. C., Gillette, C., Kesler, T., Martinelli, M., & McEvoy. M. (2006). *Units of study for teaching writing, grades 3–5*. Portsmouth, NH: Heinemann.

Chall, M. W. (2003). *Prairie train*. New York: HarperCollins.

Charney, R. S. (2002). *Teaching children to care: Classroom management for ethical and academic growth, K–8*. Turners Falls, MA: Northeast Foundation for Children.

Collins, J. L. (1998). *Strategies for struggling writers*. New York: Guilford.

Culham, Ruth. (2003). *6 + 1 traits of writing: The complete guide, grades 3 and up*. New York: Scholastic.

Fletcher, R. (1996). *Breathing in, breathing out: Keeping a writer's notebook*. Portsmouth, NH: Heinemann.

Fletcher, R. (2006). *Boy writers: Reclaiming their voices*. York, ME: Stenhouse.

Garner, B. K. (2007). *Getting to got it! Helping struggling students learn how to learn*. Alexandria, VA: ASCD.

Gee, J. P. (2007). *What video games have to teach us about learning and literacy*. New York: Palgrave Macmillan.

Giovanni, N. (2005). *Rosa*. New York: Henry Holt.

Glasswell, K. (1999). *The patterning of difference: Teachers and children constructing development in writing*. Unpublished doctoral dissertation, University of Auckland, New Zealand.

Goodman, Y. (1985). Kid watching: Observing children in the classroom. In A. Jaggar & M. T. Smith-Burke (Eds.), *Observing the language learner* (9–18). Newark, DE: International Reading Association and Urbana, IL: National Council of Teachers of English.

Graham, S., Harris, K. R., & MacArthur, C. (2006, May). Explicitly teaching struggling writers: Strategies for mastering the writing process. *Intervention in School and Clinic, 41*, 290–294.

Graham, S., & Harris, K. R. (2003). Students with learning disabilities and the process of writing: A meta-analysis of SRSD studies. In H. L. Swanson, K. R. Harris, & S. Graham (Eds.), *Handbook of learning disabilities* (pp. 323–344). New York: Guilford.

Graham, S., & Perin, D. (2007). *Writing next: Effective strategies to improve writing of adolescents in middle and high schools—A report to Carnegie Corporation of New York.* Washington, DC: Alliance for Excellent Education.

Graves, D. (2001). *The energy to teach.* Portsmouth, NH: Heinemann.

Henkes, K. (1996). *Lilly's purple plastic purse.* New York: Greenwillow.

Hesse, K. (1999). *Come on, rain!* New York: Scholastic.

Jordan, D., with Jordan, R. M. (2000). *Salt in his shoes: Michael Jordan in pursuit of a dream.* New York: Simon & Schuster.

Klinkenborg, V. (2009, January 28). John Updike. *New York Times*, p. A26.

Lane, B. (1993). *After THE END: Teaching and learning creative revision.* Portsmouth, NH: Heinemann.

Lienemann, T. O., Graham, S., Leader-Janssen, B., & Reid, R. (2006, June). Improving the writing performance of struggling writers in second grade. *Journal of Special Education, 40*(2), 66–78.

Mermelstein, L. (2007). *Don't forget to share: The crucial last step in the writing workshop.* Portsmouth, NH: Heinemann.

Munson, D. (2000). *Enemy pie.* San Francisco: Chronicle Books.

Obama, B. H. (2009). Presidential Inaugural Address, January 20, 2009. http://www.npr.org/templates/story/story.php?storyId=99590481

Owocki, G., & Goodman, Y. M. (2002). *Kidwatching: Documenting children's literacy development.* Portsmouth, NH: Heinemann.

Peterson, R. (1992). *Life in a crowded place: Making a learning community.* Portsmouth, NH: Heinemann.

Portalupi, J., & Fletcher, R. (2004). *Teaching the qualities of writing.* Portsmouth, NH: Heinemann.

Ray, K. W. (2002). *What you know by heart: How to develop curriculum for your writing workshop.* Portsmouth, NH: Heinemann.

Ray, K. W. (2006). *Study driven: A framework for planning units of study in the writing workshop.* Portsmouth, NH: Heinemann.

Routman, R. (2008). *Teaching essentials: Expecting the most and getting the best from every learner, K–8.* Portsmouth, NH: Heinemann.

Schaefer, L. M., & Miller, H. L. (2008). *Look behind! Tales of animal ends.* New York: Greenwillow.

Smith, F. (1988). *Joining the literacy club: Further essays into education.* Portsmouth, NH: Heinemann.

Snowball, D., & Bolton, F. (1999). *Spelling K–8*. York, ME: Stenhouse.

Spandel, V. (2008). *Creating writers through 6-trait writing: Assessment and instruction* (5th ed.). Upper Saddle River, NJ: Allyn & Bacon.

Swanson, S. M. (2008). *The house in the knight*. New York: Houghton Mifflin.

Tannen, D. (1988). Hearing voices in conversation, fiction, and mixed genres. In D. Tannen (Ed.), *Linguistics in context: Connecting observation and understanding* (pp. 89–114). Norwood, NJ: Ablex.

Tomlinson, C. A. (1999). *The differentiated classroom: Responding to the needs of all learners*. Alexandria, VA: ASCD.

Tomlinson, C. A. (2004). *How to differentiate instruction in mixed-ability classrooms* (2nd ed.). Alexandria, VA: ASCD.

Tomlinson, C. A., & McTighe, J. (2006). *Integrating differentiated instruction + understanding by design*. Alexandria, VA: ASCD.

Troia, G. A., Lin, S. C., Monroe, B. W., & Cohen, S. (2009). The effect of writing workshop instruction on the performance and motivation of good and poor writers. In G. A. Troia (Ed.), *Instruction and assessment for struggling writers: Evidence-based practices* (pp. 77–112). New York: Guilford.

White, E. B. (1980). *Charlotte's web*. New York: HarperCollins.

Wilde, S. (2007). *Spelling strategies and patterns: What kids need to know*. Portsmouth, NH: Heinemann.

Wormeli, R. (2006). *Fair isn't always equal: Assessing and grading in the differentiated classroom*. York, ME: Stenhouse.

Wormeli, R. (2007). *Differentiation: From planning to practice*. York, ME: Stenhouse.

Notes